AF610505

Through Hazel Eyes

Stacy Rose Bowen

ISBN: 978-1-4834-0296-3 (sc)
ISBN: 978-1-4834-0295-6 (e)

Library of Congress Control Number: 2013919513

Lulu Publishing Services rev. date: 01/16/2014

Contents

Travel

For Grammy

Grandparents are a delightful blend of laughter, caring deeds, wonderful stories, and love.—Unknown

For Bubba

Stepfathers at times are no less than those of blood; you've proved this to be true. You may not have given me the life I live, but you've become a person I look up to. It takes more than a seed to help things grow; it takes time, patience, and care. You've always given me these things and more; I thank you for always being there.—Unknown

For Carmen and Jan

"You gain strength, courage and confidence by every experience in which you really stop to look fear in the face."—Eleanor Roosevelt

Acknowledgments

I want to recognize my Savior for seeing me through the past few years, and all the difficult times in my life. I am grateful to finally write and publish a book, a desire of mine since childhood. My hope is that the contents of this book are entertaining, helpful, and inspiring to my readers.

To anyone who was involved in the stories included in these pages, named or unnamed, positive or negative, your influence has aided in my growth and evolution as a person.

Matt: We've been through hell and back several times. Half of the stories in this book wouldn't exist without you or your family. (Is that a good thing or a bad thing?)

Erik: You were with me at the starting line and always in my corner. You are my history and present—here's to the future. Cheers!

Dad: Thanks for being my sounding board, for our long discussions, and for your faith in my abilities.

To my friends and family: Your support, inspiration, encouragement, and confidence in me have provided the nudges I needed to keep pursuing this project. You knew I had something to say and wouldn't allow me to give up.

Rodger: Thank you for your proofreading and feedback.

Introduction

I have tried my best to give an accurate description of the people and events included in this memoir. At times, I have shortened or combined details because of story length or changed a name for privacy's sake (noted by an asterisk). Other than those exceptions, the memories I relay to you are my own and presented from my perspective only.

There is nothing scarier to a writer than a blank page when there are feelings to be unleashed. Whether it's a poem or a short story, to create order of jumbled thoughts is a challenge. Some of the passages in this book were simply a joy to write; my fingers and brain couldn't work fast enough. For others, I was choosy with every phrase, taking a torturously long time to convey the facts and feelings I have held close for so long.

Each chapter has its own vibe, voice, or view, with an insight into events I have encountered. Perhaps you may relate to one or several.

Family

Chapter 1

From Shy to Stacy

I was a shy child, and I hated it.

The worst part was when other people pointed it out, as if to make some sort of example out of me. It drove me nuts and contributed to the low self-esteem that haunted me for years. Both Mom and Dad were guilty of criticizing me for it. I liked to stay indoors and read, even in the summer when other kids were active and getting tan. In school, I always had a few close friends but was never Miss Popular. My reticence wouldn't have been a big deal to me if others had not so adamantly and repeatedly pointed it out. I couldn't hold a normal conversation with people because I felt what I wanted to say had little to no value and I was being secretly critiqued for every word.

For the first three years of elementary school, I had wonderful, warm young teachers and felt comfortable participating in class and in Brownies after school. During the latter half of my elementary school days, I was subjected to the tutelage of older ladies who were grumpy and had obviously lost their passion for teaching. They scared the crap out of me almost daily—intentionally, it seemed. School was pure torture those three years, and I had my first real taste of anxiety. I did *not* want to be called on or participate in class in any way. I wanted to be a wallflower and absorb the lessons like a sponge.

Middle school was terrifying for me. Not only did I attend school in a highly rated and super-snooty district, but I was also the daughter of a single mother (my parents divorced when I was just four years old), which at that time and place was not as common and accepted as it is today. Although I tried to pass as middle class, based on our income we were poor. I was very ashamed of this and powerless to change it. Imagine a thirteen-year-old with braces, clothes that weren't brand-name, living in apartments (not houses), rarely able to go to the mall, movies, or anywhere fun, and you've got yourself a loner. For years, I had a crush on a boy, but I was too insecure to tell him. Instead, I kept him at arm's length as a friend. The occasional cruel teacher who loved to embarrass and pick on me had me in knots for the entire semester (a certain English teacher stands out in my mind).

Mom moved us to a different school district between middle and high school, to a more working-class type of community. For an introvert like me, a big change like that was not easy. After a few weeks, however, I made some casual friends, and in a few months, some close ones. It took me a while to decide if I liked others and could trust them. My grades were still average, but most of the time I didn't feel socially threatened like I had at the other district. I worked on the school newspaper one semester, which included conducting interviews. This was a big step for me. My shyness kept me from participating in sports, though—and it wasn't like my mom had the funds for that anyway. Missing out on such clubs stunted my social skills even more.

My freshman year, the track coach caught sight of me running in physical-education class and told my teacher I had a great stride and he wanted me to join the team. I walked into the locker room one afternoon to join practice, but after hearing the girls inside laugh while they were changing clothes, I suddenly felt nauseated and left the building. No track for Stacy. And boy, do I regret it. The one sports activity I pursued was powder-puff football my junior year. I knew nothing about football, I didn't understand what "downs" or "scrimmage" meant, and practice was rather boring (my position was a right end). But the high I felt on the field on game night is one of my fondest memories, even if the coach only put me in the game for one play. To this day, my jersey is in my childhood memory box. The white breathable material has yellowed, but the burgundy screened print with my name and number haven't deteriorated one bit.

Becoming a teenager for me included breaking away from my mom. I grew opinionated and mouthy, and I got grounded frequently. Although I never touched drugs or alcohol, I swore like a sailor and got into other trouble with a few buddies. A lot of what my mother did or said I thought was just plain stupid, and I'd get punished for "calling her out." I was searching for my own voice and identity, one that didn't involve her and her narcissistic ways. I read *My Mother My Self.* I am sure the at-home, overly boisterous Stacy was meant to contradict the mild-acting student at school. To merge the two, to have them coexist, was a concept I would spend years working on.

Even though I had a weak voice and poor projection, I enrolled in basic choir my senior year of high school. (I needed some electives to fill up my class schedule). As a result, my low alto voice grew stronger. I was able to read and stay on the notes (even reaching high C), and I enjoyed the camaraderie with my classmates, who were mostly freshmen. There were several levels of choir classes, and even though as a senior I was a beginner, friends from my graduating class were in other levels. I quickly learned that the choir clan was accepting, warm, and fun. I came to care less about how I sounded (though I always tried my best) and just enjoy the involvement and growth experiences. It also felt good to be in the front row at the two choir concerts we performed that year.

When I was sixteen, I stopped attending the family church and started going to one where a friend belonged. This infuriated my mother and thus gave me great pleasure. The people at my new church were more accepting of others, warm, and welcoming. I became involved with the youth choir, which had about seventy members at its peak. Even if I was having an off day or my voice was worn out from singing so hard, I enjoyed being part of a group of young people who sang with purpose. The choir visited other churches for rallies, sometimes out of state. Man, were those bus trips legendary! I knew that even if I was still a bit shy, God didn't care how bad I sounded.

I did not go straight from high school to college. No adult ever presented the community college setting as a possibility for my future. My high-school grades and ACT score were less than stellar, and there was no possibility of a scholarship to a four-year institution. No one explained FAFSA to me. (Thanks a lot, guidance counselors!) So I did what silly nineteen-year-old girls do: marry the first man they fall for. I met Matthew through church, and we dated all too briefly. My twenties were spent working full-time, moving three times, and settling into a mundane life in the suburbs—sans children and white picket fence, but complete with a black Labrador and a pocketful of dreams.

I started working immediately out of high school. All of the positions I held required a high level of customer service. At first I was paranoid, shying away from that specific duty. I would volunteer to file, do inventory, or take on any odd task to avoid contact with strangers. Mostly, I worked in the finance and legal sectors. These were probably the worst areas for someone like me to provide assistance. Customers would complain, become irate, call me names, and swear at me—and being the sensitive soul I was, I took it personally. I couldn't handle their verbal abuse and idiocy. (I had enough of that growing up with my mother.) My cheeks would become flushed and hot, my blood pressure would rise, and my voice would shake after taking such lashings. After eighteen years serving the public, I backed away.

Enrolling in and attending college at thirty was a very scary challenge for me to face. No woman in my small family had obtained anything higher than a high-school diploma. My dad and uncle were the only family members with degrees (from graduate school, to boot). I didn't really view their academic accomplishments as undue pressure to succeed; rather, they were motivators, and I knew I would be proud of my own success once I completed my coursework.

Probably 75 percent of the student body at the community college was eighteen- to twenty-five-year-olds—infants, in my book. I felt out of place, afraid of the unknown, confused by the maze of old, brown brick buildings, and worried about what kind of student I would be as an adult. College is totally different from high school. No one is there to hold your hand; your fate is entirely up to you. The professors don't care if you have poor attendance, fail to turn in assignments, or flunk a test. (Well, the good ones care, but they are few.) So when I was informed that class participation ranged from 10 to 25 percent of a final class grade, I grew terrified of being challenged to step it up. This scared the crap out of me for my first few classes. Again, I was afraid that what I said in class would be wrong, that it would have no value, or that I'd get snickered at.

Then I figured out how to semi-fake it. Unless the professor was a grumpy tyrant (and there were a few), I tried to give the necessary participation. If I was too timid to raise a question or share something during class, I would make a point of chatting with the professor quickly before or after class, hoping that would somehow show him or her that I was, in fact, interested in the class content.

A few professors stand out as not only having interesting classes but also being excellent at their profession. They pushed my writing, critical-thinking, time-management, and social skills. I became comfortable with a few teachers—like John Corbin who taught me art history/appreciation and, over several semesters, became a mentor and a friend. I used his small, cluttered office as a study room on test days; while he was preparing his lecture, I would silently quiz myself. Other days we would just chat before class.

I got used to seeing certain students in more than one of my classes, and I eventually settled in. I was definitely venturing out of the safety zone I had created. I felt myself slowly morphing into a better me—yet it also felt like I was "coming home" to myself. After a few semesters, I began to stride around campus like I owned the place. Where on earth did *that* comfortable confidence come from?

I attended community college for three-and-a-half years part-time while working a full-time job. Thank goodness for my employer's tuition reimbursement program! I earned a 3.68 GPA, made the dean's list, and was a Phi Theta Kappa member. When I graduated magna cum laude in June 2009, I felt invincible. I had fought some internal demons, pushed through to my goal of a degree, and found the end result well worth it. Commencement was boring—all protocol and boring speeches—but I definitely wanted to be there. My small cheering section was there supporting my accomplishment. Once my name was called and I shook the dean's hand, I felt like my own superhero, complete with the dark green gown for my cape. When people say money can't buy happiness, they're full of crap. The tuition was worth every penny.

I was relieved that I didn't trip on the flimsy commencement stage in my heels.

If someone had told me when I was eight years old that three decades later, I would be an opinionated, soapbox-standing, accountability-seeking woman, I doubt I would have believed him or her. Today, I choose my words. I acknowledge my feelings. I'm no pushover. Most importantly, I use my voice, for better or worse. My only regret is how long it took me to find it.

Chapter 2

Transitions Don't Have to Affect Traditions

I had only been camping once or twice before, as a child, in Manistee, Michigan. Even then, my dad and his side of the family stayed in a rented mobile home on the campground instead of a tent. That grey metal box was like an oven; I swear it was 90 degrees even at night. The communal showers were the kind you had to pay money to use, like a self-service car wash. Stacy is not a Buick, so . . . I don't think so.

After Matt and I became engaged in 1994, he was so excited about my joining the Annual Bowen Family Camping Trip. His family really talked it up, but I was quite hesitant to join them for a few reasons: 1) I was not yet very well acquainted with his huge family; 2) my past experience, noted above, was not positive; and 3) I was OCD about cleanliness, and camping involves dirt.

Two months before our September wedding, we drove four hours north for a long weekend at Burt Lake State Park. Normally, the Annual was a two-week-long escape for approximately forty members of Matt's extended family. For the longest time, they went when the

Big Three automakers in Detroit were on shutdown at the beginning of July. The tradition started in 1966, with Matt's parents and cousins as the first generation to engage in this ritual outing. As the family aged and grew, the generations kept on going.

The head ranger at the park, along with two assistant rangers, got to know the clan and would recognize them every year at check-in. Other rangers would stop by the family's sites to visit and catch up.

My first experience at Burt Lake was interesting, to say the least. The state park itself was gorgeous, and the family always seemed to snag the good sites (with grass, not dirt—and away from flood zones). I was unsure if I'd packed the right camping clothes, and I did not know what the weather would be like.

Danny, Matt's big brother, was recently divorced that year but still came and brought his four children. Matt slept in Danny's large fifth-wheel camper, and I was relegated to a "girl's tent" on a cot with Danny's two daughters, my soon-to-be nieces—one of whom, Maria, allowed my cotton duffle bag to drop into the very corner of the tent that got soaked with rain the first night. Everything I brought was wet through and through. I was *very* upset. Luckily, the small town we were in had a coin Laundromat. It was less than clean-looking itself, but it was the only way to wash and dry my clothes. I think I had to go out in public in my pajamas. Doing laundry took up one complete morning.

Maria felt very bad and apologized, but since I didn't grow up with tons of relatives like the Bowens, I overreacted and believed it was a thoughtless thing to knowingly leave someone's bag sitting in the corner of the tent. (When camping, we look out for and help each other, but this was not such an example.) Making me more pissed was the fact that all the kids had Rubbermaid trunks for their stuff—obviously, so things wouldn't get wet. It would have been helpful if Matt had told me some of the important basics before we drove up for the weekend.

Another highlight of that first trip was an event that would come to be known as the "pie feet" story. Yes, again, I was a victim of my ignorance in the ways of camping. I had not packed sufficiently comfortable sandals, so Matt bought me a pair of white leather Bass Sunjuns at the Bass outlet store in West Branch. I was wearing said shoes when helping a family member transfer tents to another site one morning. (No one wanted to take the tent down and put it back up, so it was emptied and put on the bed of a pickup and driven to its new location. Ah, the odd innovations of camping.) By noon, with several peoples' assistance, the task was complete.

When I returned to my tent on Danny's site to get my beach gear, I removed my sandals, and there was a blatantly obvious pie-lattice pattern on the top of my feet in the colors of a candy cane. My feet got *that* burned by the morning sun in the matter of an hour and a half. Who gets second-degree sunburn before noon? Me with my pasty WASP skin, that's who. I practically jumped out of my skin when I applied green aloe gel to the burn.

Still shy around the clan, I dreaded people seeing my feet. They had a saying about camping, that "there are no sacred cows." If someone did something funny or stupid, he or she got teased for the rest of the trip at the nightly campfires, and often for years afterward. There was no way to avoid displaying this unusual and unintentional foot art, and the "pie feet" story went down in the history books of Bowen camping. Initiation complete.

Campfires each evening were a whole new experience for me as well. All of the cousins congregated onto Danny's site, bringing their lawn chairs and food to cook. If the campsite was near the water, it could get very chilly at night; even if it was 87, sunny, and humid during the day, it could easily be 54 and breezy come sundown. Pants, hoodies, and sometimes blankets were required. As people gathered at Danny's spot, the circle of people and chairs around the fire pit grew larger, the chatter rose in volume, and the cooking of bratwursts, hot dogs, and s'mores began. There were informal competitions regarding method and timing. It was a big deal to cook the perfect brat or not burn a marshmallow.

Sometimes the clan got pretty rowdy, retelling funny family stories, and the young night-shift rangers would walk by and give us a warning about quiet time at eleven. Eventually cousins and friends packed up their gear and headed back to their sites after hours of laughing, eating, and stargazing. Some would make it to one in the morning. Something about being at camp in the night makes one realize how small we all are and what a big universe there is. Leaving Danny's site, our clothes would smell like campfire, a smell that is now one of my favorites.

Mornings during camping, family members took their time waking up, making breakfast, and brewing coffee. It was vacation—there was no rush. We sprinted for the WC/bathhouses to empty that bursting bladder. This had to be timed well, because each of the four building units were cleaned by the rangers (ugh, I'd hate that job) at a certain hour of the day, but never all at once. So if you headed toward the potty closest to your site only to find it closed for cleaning, you were forced to sprint to one down the road. One of the biggest accomplishments of the day was getting that first bathroom trip in, I swear!

Every soul wandering the park roads had the same groggy eyes and bed-head, and was still in pajamas, whether on foot or bicycle. Strangers said good morning or nodded in acknowledgement. Once one was no longer concerned about bladder or bowel issues, senses slowly awakened to the park coming to life: boat motors on the lake, kids waking up, bacon cooking, and the smell of campfires from the previous night.

The majority of the family came to the beach area every day. We claimed a section away from the park's main beach where it was less crowded. Any and every beach accessory got dragged there: floaties, chairs, towels, coolers, books, magazines, radio. Approximately six hours of the day were spent at the beach if the weather held out (and the lake wasn't too cold). I found peace lying on my towel, drifting in and out of sleep, my senses aware of the smells of Coppertone and boat fuel and the sounds of seagulls squawking, the lake water rippling along the shore, and faint music. Quite the Zen experience.

Despite the pie feet and saturated clothing, I came to realize there were benefits to this annual tradition. The detachment from work and world events and having to live with a minimum of basics definitely grabbed my attention. Perhaps I could become a Bowen camper after all . . .

The following year, 1995, Matt and I bought a 1984 Coleman pop-up camper for $800 at a garage sale. It was an unusual specimen, as only one end popped out, for a full-size bed. It was probably the smallest pop-up ever made. The outer canvas and interior fabric were in great condition (if you're into brown and orange, which I wasn't, but still . . .). Since it had the unique feature of only one pop-out bed, for some reason it acquired the name of "the Polish trailer" (no offense to the Polish community intended). The Coleman was a step up from a tent, but barely.

Our nephew Timmy set a family record that year: at Soody's restaurant near Mackinaw City, he ate a seventy-two-ounce sirloin dinner, a challenge which, upon completion, made his dinner free (kind of like in *Uncle Buck*). Usually the family went to the restaurant for a simple Friday fish dinner, but Timmy, being fourteen and obstinate, and having an ego and metabolic rate larger than normal, decided he was the man for the challenge. He was the youngest person to complete the meal and, as champion, he was awarded a hat and boxers ("Home of the 72-ouncer" on the front panel—nice) and had a Polaroid picture taken and nailed to the "wall of honor" by the waitress. The restaurant has since changed owners a few times and we no longer go there. Surely the pictures are gone. But it is yet another bookmarked occasion that would be included in Bowen camping lore for years to come.

Although the Polish trailer served its purpose, Matt and I wanted more space, especially since a black Labrador named Storm had become part of our family. In early 1996, we bought an eighteen-foot travel trailer for a steal as a result of a bidding war at a local RV show. Matt's parents bought the Polish trailer and used it that summer. The following year, the family played a round of musical campers: Matt and I purchased a twenty-six-foot Mallard camper with a slide-out by trading in our other trailer; his folks bought a top-of-the-line Coleman pop-up; and our nephew Daryl* bought his grandparents' Polish camper. People get caught up in upgrading their campers every few years like they would a car. Our Mallard, now well over ten years old, looks and works nearly as good as it did when we bought it. So until it starts falling apart, we're keeping the duck.

In September of 1998, my niece Theresa (Danny's oldest daughter) died in a freak accident at the home of some friends she had been running around with. Getting that phone call was surreal. The house was located near Matt's sister Debbie's home at the time, so she and her family arrived on the scene first. It was a run-down white two-story house with several young adults living there.

Our family came as soon as we all could. The police and coroner wouldn't allow access into the house. So for three or four hours on a pleasant fall evening, we stood on the sidewalk, huddled together in pockets, just staring at the open doorway and crying, wondering what happened.

Watching Theresa's siblings and parents go through a myriad of feelings was awful. It kept being said, "Parents shouldn't have to bury their children; it's not natural." No, it's not, nor is it fair.

Slowly, over a period of a couple of summers, a bunch of the cousins stopped coming to Burt Lake in Indian River. In a way, it was nice—we didn't have to try to arrange our day with forty other people. But the sounds of kids playing in the shallow water or beach sand, certain people's company, boats or Sea-Doos—those were missed.

A core group evolved, about twenty people or so: Matt and me; his folks; Debbie and her husband, Tim, and their kids; and Danny and his kids. One cousin, Willie, and his wife held on too and kept returning, sometimes with their kids and/or grandkids. Willie and Danny were very close, almost like brothers, and they had the same deranged sense of humor and practical-joker personalities. It was t-r-o-u-b-l-e when they were together!

June 27, 2001, was not only the worst birthday I would ever have, but one of the saddest days of my life. On this specific Wednesday, Danny got into a fatal accident in the stake truck he drove, running into a parked semi on the side of I-75 South near Pontiac. The subsequent on-location investigation blocked traffic for hours that afternoon. Instead of Danny's parents or siblings identifying his body at the scene, a first cousin who was a captain with the sheriff's department verified that it was indeed Danny.

As family and some church folk gathered at my in-laws' house and brought food, people were concerned about our niece Maria, Danny's youngest—and by then only—daughter, who was at Cedar

Point with friends for the day. Everyone was worried about notifying her of this life-changing event upon her return home later that night. This accident was such an out-of-nowhere shock. People didn't talk much, but were rather zombielike or crying.

Camping was only a month away. Some felt strange about still going up north, like it was wrong to continue our lives, especially to enjoy one of Danny's favorite events. Others, including myself, felt we should go as usual; Danny would want that. He would feel bad if he robbed us of an opportunity for family healing. Also, he would have felt absolutely horrible about forever altering my birthday.

It was definitely a very different experience camping in 2001. There were somber times—a story (funny or sad, usually funny) would be told and the wistful expressions on people's faces spoke volumes. We had all these great, crazy memories to be retold at the campfire, and for that matter, for the rest of our lives, but Danny himself was gone. His personality was a big presence, and we were stuck with a large void.

As a kind of memorial, one day late in the vacation, Willie slow-cooked a pork loin, and we all brought a dish to his site for a potluck dinner. After we had eaten, we carried out a ceremony that I had suggested; I thought the family would think it silly, but they liked the idea. We each individually sought out a rock the size we wanted to use to write a farewell note to Danny. I bought permanent Sharpie markers at the grocery store in town. There we all sat at Willie's site in lawn chairs, thinking, holding our rocks, waiting for our turn with a marker. There was an uncomfortable silence as people thought of what to write, broken only by the stifled tears of those who were or had already written their message. When all were finished, those who wanted to made their way to the beach. There was a boat and two Sea-Doos; whoever wanted to ride out into the lake could join so long as there was room.

We grabbed the rocks and life jackets, packed the water vessels, and headed toward the middle of the lake, to a point where we knew it was quite deep. We stopped and idled all engines, holding on to each others' crafts to stay bobbing in the small waves together. We had a moment of silence, dedicated this tribute to Danny's memory, and then hurled the rocks down into the deep water of Burt Lake.

The atmosphere among us was awkward. We drove back to shore and parked on the beach. Although people were sad, they said they liked the ceremony—that it was a cool idea. My hope was that it would allow us all to say good-bye to Danny, since he was killed so unexpectedly and suddenly. Burt Lake was his favorite place, and I hope Danny somehow found our words on those rocks to keep him company.

Matt's dad, Daniel, was diagnosed with pancreatic cancer in 2000. He had taken time off from the family business to go through chemo and radiation for several months, and then he went into remission for about a year and a half. By June of 2002, Daniel was under hospice care at his home. He'd lost his desire to eat and ability to speak, and he was on morphine to ease his discomfort.

On July 12 just after midnight, with a handful of family around his hospital bed crying or singing church songs, he drew his last breath and slipped peacefully into the beyond. I had never watched anybody die before; he went so quietly. It was a lot to process. Daniel had laid in the living room with one foot on earth and one foot in heaven, and then he stepped away from us. We watched as his soul made this amazing transition while his body lay still and small. Really, it was a beautiful and amazing experience.

Again, the timing of this loss was close to the annual camping trip. What to do? After the deaths of Danny and Daniel within the past year, the family really wanted to be together as much as possible. We went ahead and made the bittersweet trek up north. So that his mother, Anna, could still go, Matt drove Daniel's truck and pulled his parents' twenty-nine-foot Coleman travel trailer (yes, they'd upgraded again) while I drove Matt's truck and pulled our Mallard. I had never done it before and was a bundle of nerves.

It wouldn't have been so bad if Matt hadn't thought it would save time upon arrival at the park if he filled our water tank before leaving home. In doing so, however, this caused the weight of the trailer to constantly shift with every twist of the highway, and it also added more weight for the truck to pull, making it harder than normal to control. Matt would use his Nextel phone to beep me and ask why I was driving so slowly. *Umm, because if I go over fifty-five, it feels like I'm gonna tip this beast over, that's why, genius!*

The family didn't have a ceremony for Daniel the way we did for Danny the previous summer. I don't recall why. Maybe because Indian River was Danny's safe place, while Daniel felt more comfortable at his cabin in the Oscoda woods. Anna had a hard time camping without her husband for the first time in forty years. Matt pulled double duty when it came to setting up and taking down both of his ladies' sites, a concern of mine because he'd had bariatric surgery and had to be extremely careful not to do anything that might lead to a hernia.

Danny had made a friend in town, back in the early 1990s perhaps. His name was Don Bowen (no relation, oddly enough). They became pals, and Don would come around when the family was camping and treat the kids to tubing on the lake with his boat, the *Love Shack*, or take the adults for evening sunset cruises down the Indian River. Through the years, he became a mainstay.

Don is severely ADD, but he's fun and one of those nice, gentlemanly types. He drove downstate for Danny's funeral and stayed at my in-laws' house. He has been nothing but kind to our family for twenty years, and he didn't have to; he could have written us off after Danny passed.

In 2011, Don and I kayaked the Sturgeon River together—quite the five-hour tour. I got dumped three times. Thank God I had tethered my paddle to my life jacket, or I'd have truly been You Know Where!

The family adjusted to the new normal of the annual camping trip, with dwindling attendance. Anna eventually sold her trailer and quit camping as she crept up in age. Debbie and Tim would come sporadically and stay in tents, their pop-up camper having fallen into disrepair. Our black Labrador, Storm, died in February of 2002, and we adopted a yellow Lab, Cooper just months after; he became our new traveling companion. Looking back, it seems so strange at times—when I first camped in 1994, I was nineteen years old and knew nothing about this hobby or the family that participated in it. Now I know a lot more than most women about the mechanics of camping.

As our nieces and nephews started making their own families, another dynamic shifted. Those punk kids who used to get in trouble for staying out too late and illegally climbing up the back side of the hill to the Cross in the Woods were now parents. Debbie's two eldest, Timmy and Tammy, are both married with four young ones between them. All three of Danny's remaining children have kids; Daryl has two and Maria and Mark each have one. And I'm sure there will be more children in the years to come (sadly, though, with no contribution from me). The Bowens have a fourth generation of Burt Lake campers in the making. Let the tradition live on, and may our departed be forever remembered.

We'll keep taking "The Gulp" (a tradition on the last day of vacation where all of us form a circle in the lake, hold hands, and bend down to take in a gulp of clear Burt Lake water) every year and think of Theresa, Danny, and Daniel as we do so.

CHAPTER 3

Relative Strangers

It's funny, as you get older you see the dynamics of other families and realize that either yours is "normal" or you envy what appears to be "normal."

My mom and her older brother were opposites from birth; they never did get along as children or even into adulthood for the most part. My Uncle Kyle* was rumored to be my grandma's favorite, and supposedly Grammy told my mom once that she was a "mistake baby." You can imagine how that affected what was an already unhealthy family situation. Legend had it Kyle would chase my mom around their house while my grandparents were at work, threatening to pour castor oil down her throat.

After Uncle Kyle met and married my Aunt Rita*, they moved to Michigan's Upper Peninsula following college graduation to start their teaching careers. Rita was from there, raised by parents who were Finnish immigrants. They decided not to have children. My mom, dad, and I had limited contact with these "black sheep of the family." If it weren't for a picture I have showing a dozen family members—four generations of our family together celebrating Christmas when I was five—I would have doubts they were even my relatives.

I recall two very fuzzy childhood memories when I spent time with my aunt and uncle. In one instance, I was three or four years old, and my parents and I drove to the Upper Peninsula for a visit during winter. They had a black Labrador I played with in their small living room, trying to ride him like a pony. Another time, not too long after, Kyle and Rita drove downstate for a visit and stayed at my grandma's house. Mom and I lived there at the time (following my parents' divorce), and I was always roaming the neighborhood on my bicycle. My aunt and uncle walked with me once as I pedaled the well-known blocks. For the first time, I felt awkward around adults. I didn't know them or remember much about them, yet they were basically my next of kin. I felt off-balance at the notion.

When I was perhaps eight years old, my grandma, mother, and I packed into Grammy's light blue 1970s Impala and drove to Denver, Colorado, where Kyle and Rita had moved. We took three days to make a trip that should have taken no more than two. I read on the backseat floor, stretched out, so I wouldn't get carsick. I enjoyed keeping track of where we were on state maps and reading all the license plates and exit signs. Multiple Stuckey's stops were made.

Kyle and Rita had a condo in the suburbs; he was a policeman at the time, and she was in telemarketing. They had at least one cat as a pet, and I was assigned to sleep on the floor of their extra bedroom since I was youngest. Mom and Grams shared the bed. I was allergic to the cat hair embedded in the carpet, so every morning I awoke with puffy eyes, a stuffy nose, and a cottony throat.

My first experience with my uncle's nasty temper came one day when I was looking for something in the kitchen drawers. Kyle walked into the kitchen as I unknowingly opened the drawer in which he kept his off-duty pistol, and he blew up at me. I ended up crying and going to the spare bedroom in fear and shame. I think my mom in turn yelled at him. How would I have a clue there was a loaded gun in the house?

He never warned us. Plus, he wasn't my parent; I hardly knew him. It wasn't his place to reprimand me in that manner.

My second experience with his temper came during that same Colorado trip. Uncle Kyle drove the three of us to the Rocky Mountains, stopping at Loveland Pass and the Continental Divide. It was so cool (pun intended) to play in snow when it was 60 degrees and sunny! At one point during the drive, a bee got in the car via an open window, and I started screaming from the backseat about it. Bees were a *huge* fear of mine as a kid; my mom had programmed me into believing I was possibly allergic to them. My uncle went off on a tirade then too, yelling at me for yelling about the bee. My mom had to explain that I was afraid of bees, and although I shouldn't have freaked out as much as I did, he shouldn't have yelled at a little girl for being afraid of a bee.

When I was thirteen years old, my mom purchased a one-way plane ticket to Denver, Colorado; she thought it a good idea for me to stay with Uncle Kyle and Aunt Rita for a few weeks. I was glad to get away from the drama in our house that summer (Mom had remarried and I hated my stepdad), yet skeptical about being alone with these relatives I still barely knew and had not-so-fond memories of.

At the time of my trip, Kyle was off work and packing up their condo; they were preparing to move out of state. Rita was at her office five days a week. So the man who more or less terrified me was to be my babysitter, entertainment director, and tour guide. My aunt and uncle have always been very active, so on weekends the three of us went on hiking excursions in the mountains. I was, up until this point, an "indoor girl" who read and watched TV and did not break a sweat; it seemed very unfeminine. (So did peeing outside while facing uphill, but that's another story.) Climbing for seven hours was hard work, what with all the switchbacks, boulder-climbing, and stream-crossing. Did I mention I was there in June and July? Holy hell it was hot!

I didn't journal my trip or even take many pictures, which is *so* not like me. Looking back, I feel rather bad for my uncle, who had to provide daily entertainment to a teenage girl he barely knew. There were days we didn't really do much, which was fine but odd. I liked being on the go, seeing all the sights. Kyle was an interesting guide, as he hated typical touristy spots and seemed to know all the background information of places, so some of what we did was not on the average tourists' agenda.

We went to the Jolly Rancher candy factory, where the public could buy the hard candy in bulk, and there were flavors there not sold in stores. I was literally a kid in a candy store, and it was hard to choose what to buy! Decisions, decisions . . . I bought a large bag of pink-lemonade candy (so good!) that I enjoyed for weeks. We also visited the site of Celestial Seasonings tea company.

One whole day he led me on a bike tour of Boulder—I rode Rita's bike, which fit me perfectly, as she was a petite woman. We whizzed through the streets, sidewalks, and bike paths of the college town on a beautiful sunny day. He showed me the house that was used for the TV show *Mork and Mindy*. We walked some of the University of Colorado campus and visited the bookstore. I wanted to buy something with the buffalo mascot on it, but didn't want to carry it awkwardly the rest of the day on the bike. We walked Pearl Street Mall.

Another day, Kyle took me to a baseball game for Denver's minor league at the former Mile High Stadium. Rather than purchase stale peanuts at the field, we stopped at a grocery store on the way to buy "real" fresh peanuts and took those to the game instead. I also got to visit downtown Denver, but don't recall much other than the Foucault Pendulum display.

I must give Kyle props: on my fourteenth birthday, he took me to a New Kids on the Block/Tiffany concert at Red Rocks Amphitheater. We had lawn tickets, and were at the back of the hill, but I was thrilled to be there! Poor man—I'm sure he wanted to be *anywhere* but around 20,000 screaming teenage girls. He printed out a custom-made birthday banner for me on their home computer and hung it in the condo. Very thoughtful of Uncle Kyle (although perhaps it was Aunt Rita's idea).

Their neighbor over the fence had a new litter of puppies, and I visited them a few times, loving their soft fur and wriggly bodies. On several days, Kyle and I went to the community pool at their condo complex. I was so glad for the refreshing water! It felt rather odd being in a bathing suit in front of Kyle, and it seemed odd seeing him in one. I *was* an awkward fourteen-year-old, after all. I stayed in the water most of the time to avoid being around him much.

Another thing I was uncomfortable about was eating dinner. Uncle Kyle was a strict clean-plate-club member, so even if I didn't like what was prepared or wasn't that hungry, I *had* to eat the portions doled out to me. Otherwise he would throw a minor fit and force-feed me like I was a two-year-old.

Perhaps the best thing about my three-week visit—other than the awesome experiences of hiking in the Rockies and Boulder's Flatirons—were the evenings, after dinner, when the three of us sat on the upstairs deck off their bedroom, face our chairs west, and watch the summer sun slowly meet the tips of the foothills before disappearing, leaving a lingering peach glow. Kyle and Rita would have a nightcap or two, and I was even allowed to sip some beer.

When Kyle seemed to be running out of activities, I decided it was time to leave. So I spoke with my mom, she purchased a return ticket, and I picked it up from the travel agent near the complex. Even though I dreaded going home, I didn't want to overstay my welcome, either, and I sensed I was coming close to it. But when it came time to say good-bye at the airport, I was sad. In a way, the three of us had developed a semi-routine, and I was getting used to it. I wished Rita could have been home more to do stuff with; she was shy like me but knew how to handle Kyle's mood swings. I had enough of those to deal with at home with my mother.

In the late 1990s, I took five days and flew by myself to Omaha, which was about thirty minutes west of Kyle and Rita's new house in Iowa. There was nothing in Iowa I particularly wanted to see, I just needed to get away, see someplace new, and escape my boring Michigan life for a short spell. I hadn't seen them in about ten years.

When the puddle-jumper of a plane landed in Omaha, I was supposed to look for Uncle Kyle and Aunt Rita by the gate (this was pre-9/11 when that was still allowed by the TSA). I did not see them there, so I figured if nothing else, I would surely meet up with them at baggage claim. So I walked over and waited for my suitcase and relatives to appear. Surprisingly, Kyle wasn't super mad when they located me at baggage claim insisting they were at the gate as we agreed.

Their house was literally in the middle of rolling corn and soy fields, with occasional cattle herds. They owned a few acres, with a garden out back where my uncle grew hops for his homemade beer. Approximately one dozen fruit trees scattered the yard. A huge pole barn stored my uncle's tractor and *many* tools. Their ranch house didn't have air-conditioning, and as it happened, there was a crazy heat streak while I was there—in the nineties in May! It was difficult to fall asleep at night in the stagnant heat, but I loved having the casement windows open and listening to crickets and bullfrogs.

One day, Rita took a day off work and took me to Doorly Zoo in Omaha, since she knew I loved animals. I recall a butterfly house and also a tropical rainforest building. She made a comment about not liking kids—they made her uncomfortable. I thought it odd, but I also felt some familiarity with the sentiment.

Kyle took me rambling around the Iowa countryside in his pickup truck the day after a tornado hit nearby, though I think he wanted to assess the damage more than show me farmland. We stopped in a quaint town with an actual town square, something you read about but don't imagine really still exists until you see it for yourself. We ate lunch at a diner that I believe was an old railroad car, or made to look like one. I have very few pictures and no journal to jog my memory.

Although that visit was brief in comparison to the Colorado trip, as before, at the airport I found it difficult to say good-bye. What was my attachment to these people? They were formal, and not warm like family *should* be. I didn't know them really well, even after two visits. They were both like clams—hard to open up. We hugged good-bye at my departure gate, and they walked away while I sat for a short while until it was time to board the puddle-jumper back to Michigan.

I think it was probably another ten years before I saw them again. They came to Michigan to visit Grammy. I was very close to her, so I drove to her apartment the day they visited. They had just recently traveled to Ireland, and as Kyle, Rita, and I took a walk around Gram's small town, they regaled me with tales of kissing the Blarney Stone; enduring the wet, cool weather; driving through the green fields; and drinking good beer.

The next time I saw Kyle was just after Grammy died in 2006. He and Rita stayed with my mom and her third husband, Wayne, at their home up north the week Grammy was going downhill. My aunt stayed a few days, and then she had to return to Iowa for work. I only saw my uncle at the church for Grammy's same-day viewing and funeral. He is notoriously unemotional except when losing his temper, but for this event he was almost rudely antisocial. I was beside myself with grief, having lost one of my best friends, and he walked around robotically stoic. I knew Grammy best, yet it was Kyle who spoke a brief eulogy. I was jealous but also a hyperventilating mess of waterworks in the front pew.

Not long after Grammy passed, Kyle and Rita sold their Iowa home and moved to Michigan's northern Lower Peninsula. Kyle officially retired, and Rita worked two more years remotely for her longtime employer. They bought a beautiful Cape Cod–style house in a small clearing off a god-awful dirt road—inaccessible, almost. (A metaphor for their personalities, perhaps?) Matt and I visited for a long weekend their first summer there. Matt's nephew, Mark, lived and worked in the area, so it was a two-for-one trip. I fell in love with downtown Traverse City, and the Leelanau and Old Mission Peninsulas were home to several local and delicious wineries with plenty of free taste-testing.

I also visited my aunt and uncle's northern hideaway twice by myself, and I was surprisingly much more comfortable around them both. I think in part it was due to "finding myself" a bit in college combined with the assertiveness I gained while dealing with Matt's medical trauma (see chapter 5), but I was no longer intimidated by Kyle or his temper. I was at an age when I knew that I was not the one responsible for his mood swings, therefore I more or less blew them off. *He* was in control of his reactions, not me.

The best time I've shared with them to date was after they bought a winter condo near Phoenix, Arizona. I visited a few months after they were more or less settled in, in March of 2010. It was a five-day stay, and honestly, it was nowhere near long enough. I actually had fun with them! Kyle has a very sarcastic sense of humor, I discovered, and once in a while, I was able to tease him back for all the times he made me feel miniscule. Of course, his face revealed next to nothing, sometimes a slight smirk. Rita and I really clicked—over pets, clothes, activities, and Kyle's oddball-ness. We had a girl's day and rode public transit into Phoenix to visit the Heard Museum, which was very effective in its arrangement of the artifacts to increase one's knowledge of the southwest Native American population of the United States. We enjoyed a savory Tex-Mex lunch in the museum courtyard under the midday sun, among statues and plants. We met Kyle for beers late that afternoon at a local brewpub on the way back to their condo.

Another day, Kyle, Rita, her college girlfriend, and I went for a six-hour hike in the Superstition Mountains. It was nice to be hiking in non-humid seventy-degree weather instead of sticky ninety degrees like back in Denver twenty years earlier. As an older hiker, I was able to really appreciate the vast and magnificent surroundings. I had to remind myself to look up from the uneven trail and take in the beautiful rock formations and plants surrounding me. Each step seemed to reveal a new view, and I made myself turn around, as that view changed with every step as well. I snapped pictures nonstop, but I also paused to just stand still and take in the moment. I had told my hiking companions that if I lagged a few hundred feet behind them, I would catch up.

Being under the vast blue sky surrounded by such rugged and open beauty was almost a spiritual experience for me. Some people feel closest to God in a church with four walls and stained glass. I feel Him closest when I am out in nature, especially in a setting like that, where one can't help but appreciate His creations and realize how small one is in the scheme of things.

On yet another perfect sunny Arizona spring day, Kyle and Rita took me to the Desert Botanical Garden. A lime green Dale Chihuly glass installation greeted visitors at the entrance. Kyle had always been into science, so after we walked around and learned the many varieties of cacti, we conversationally quizzed each other. "Isn't that a cool prickly pear species?" Many had the oddest shapes or characteristics, so they were easy to remember and most picture-worthy. Papago Peak loomed in the background.

We had a snack instead of lunch and tried to find a table with an umbrella to hide from the sun. On our way back to the condo, we stopped at a hole-in-the wall pub for a cold one. Kyle and Rita actually seemed relaxed and talked quite freely in front of me. They even shared why they were glad they never had children. That scenario was so different from our early years together.

The most recent sighting of my aunt and uncle was at my stepfather, Wayne's, memorial service, after he passed on. Church is not their thing *at all.* I'm not sure if they're agnostic or what; I've never asked them. But I think yes. While my mom fluttered around the church acting improperly fake, the four of us sat in the front row, awkwardly and stoically waiting for the memorial to begin. For this memorial, I *did* get up to speak a few words about how special Wayne was to me, and Matt did too. Wayne was a great father figure; he never made me feel like a stepchild. At the noisy and crowded church banquet afterward, our shrinking family sat together quietly.

I have tried to keep in some sort of contact with Kyle and Rita via e-mail the past few years. Usually if I don't instigate correspondence, I don't hear from them. We usually receive their Christmas card last-minute, like they figure they should mail one to us since we sent one to them. It has always seemed so awkward to me to have such close kin seem like strangers. It's truly sad. I don't know why they've always been distant; it could trace back to Kyle's relationship with my mom from their childhood. Perhaps he thought I was like his sister, and he didn't want to deal with her "Mini Me." But my personality, sense of humor, ambition, and hobbies are totally different from my mom's. At least with Kyle and Rita, I share an interest in hiking, kayaking, reading, travel, and culture.

Sometimes I wonder if it's worth it, to be the one always putting in the effort to remain in contact. How do they feel about me? I broke through the emotional barrier and was brave enough to ask recently. I was disappointed by their response—or rather, the lack thereof. They remain strangers to me.

Unconsciously for the most part, I have taken the less-than-great example Uncle Kyle and Aunt Rita set for me and turned it around within myself. I have seven nieces and nephews, plus eight grand-nieces and nephews. The older set were difficult for me to establish myself as an adult aunt figure with, since many are close to my age and I joined the family in their early teens. Sometimes there were sibling-like arguments. As we all grew up, they became more like my cousins. With their children, though, I feel I really am Aunt Stacy. Each child is individual in personality and has his or her own place in my heart. I have changed their diapers, played with them, baby-sat, and vacationed with them.

Since I don't have any children of my own, I am grateful for any time spent with this younger generation. They grow so fast. Realizing how much I enjoy those little boys' and girls' role in my life, I am also acutely aware of what my aunt and uncle missed out on by putting up fences—and what I missed out on, too. I hope none of my little nieces and nephews ever feel the way I did while growing up. I do not want to be a stranger to them.

Chapter 4

Memory Lane

I lost two of the most important people in my life to Alzheimer's—my maternal grandmother and my stepfather. I would like to introduce you to two wonderful people I have been blessed to call family.

Marge Pratt was born in 1919 and resided in Genesee County, Michigan her entire life. She got married, had two children, and worked full time as a clothes/retail clerk. She became a widow in her mid-fifties. I was ten months old when my grandfather passed, so I never knew him. When I was five, my parents divorced, and the first year after that, my mother and I lived with Grammy so Mom could pull herself together. I loved living in Grammy's older brick home in (what used to be) one of the best neighborhoods in Flint. By this time, Grammy had retired and I had morning kindergarten, so the afternoons were 'our' time.

Grammy used to work election events, and she would bring unused pads of pink registration slips home with her. I would sit at her desk pretending to be some important businesswoman, scribbling fake names and instructions on them. She taught me how to ride my bicycle without training wheels. I was allowed to ride my Big Wheel in the street, all over the neighborhood, rounding up friends and playing with lightning bugs in the evenings. Looking back, it's a crazy notion—a five-year-old and her pals running the streets of Flint alone—but that was probably the best year of my childhood. I was actually allowed to be a kid.

After Mom and I moved out of Grammy's house, Mom started a yearly moving tradition, constantly finding a better or cheaper apartment in the area. I was raised as a gypsy, basically; I wasn't attached to too many of my belongings, but the things I was connected to were hands-off! Ironically, I was a sentimentalist. After a year or two of our musical-apartment game, Grams sold her house (she didn't want to deal with the upkeep anymore) and began following us to whatever new rental neighborhood we moved to. This was handy for Mom, because Grams became a built-in babysitter after school and on sick days, as well as my school chauffer and entertainment for the summer.

The times Grams looked after me became some of my most cherished memories. After school, she would pick me up and take me back to her one-bedroom apartment, and she would always have snacks to give me while I did homework at the dining-room table. Faygo and molasses cookies or Cheetos—yum! She was very willing and able to help with me with a variety of homework assignments, from social studies to math to spelling. I would open up to her about my day and discuss friends, teachers, and crushes.

When I was sick, Grams picked me up from school or my apartment, pulled out her sofa bed, put clean sheets on it, threw a granny-square blanket over me, and brought me pop and soup in between my naps and watching *Little House on the Prairie* and her CBS soap operas. As I got older, in my middle-school years, I chose to stay home alone, but knowing she was a phone call away was reassuring.

I fondly remember summers as the best time spent with her. Not many eight-year-olds would enjoy meeting their grandmother's girlfriends for breakfast at seven thirty once a week, but I didn't mind. Those women became kind of like my adopted great-aunts, which I loved, coming from a small nuclear family. I listened quietly while they gossiped over coffee. Ben Franklin (the craft store) was still in business back then, and since I would read Gram's or Mom's *Family Circle* magazines, if there was a craft I wanted to try, Gram and I would trot off to get the supplies I needed. In fact, through the years, I acquired a large craft box that she kept in her storage closet. It was full of coloring books, stickers, crayons, markers, chalk, glue, scissors, felt, yarn—you name it. I could *never* use the line "I'm bored" with her!

Grammy was a dutiful daughter to her own mother. My ninety-something great-grandma was in a nursing home, and although it scared the crap out of me to go, I accompanied Grams almost every week as her companion. I never spoke much, as I was uncomfortable in the convalescent-home environment at my young age. I remember that Grams brought her mom pink candy mints every week, the color of Pepto-Bismol, and the two of them would sit by the window in her room and try to talk. Great-grandma was losing her hearing and sight, and over the years it became difficult to communicate with her. After about an hour's visit, we would leave. I remember the strong smell of urine penetrating the air of the hallways; I tried not to gag. As a reward for tolerating this weekly trip, Grams always treated me to an ice-cream cone afterward.

When I became a teenager, we no longer lived in the same neighborhood as Grams, and some distance grew between us, which I suppose is natural for a teen trying to individuate from family members. When I got poor grades or detention, she was disappointed but didn't scold me like Mom would. Sure, I made her cry a few times. Disappointing her broke my heart a little. I knew she loved me no matter what I did, though, which is not something I could say about my mom.

After I married at age nineteen, I drove to Grammy's apartment (now in a highrise for seniors only) on random Saturdays when the weather was decent. By this time, she pretty much relied on a walker, one with yellow tennis balls on the legs. Depending on her arthritis, I'd take her out to lunch and Kmart; she loved running about, even if she wasn't feeling up to par. I was glad to put in a little time doing something for her, since she did so much for me growing up. Mom had moved a few hours away to northern Michigan and then to Florida, so she rarely saw Grams, and neither did my uncle, who lived in Iowa. I think Grams was secretly sad to be so alone in her golden years. I wish I could have done more to keep her company.

By the time my mom moved back to Michigan, Gram's health was going downhill. She had undergone open heart surgery, was having kidney issues, a bout with shingles, loss of appetite, and signs of dementia were setting in. Mom placed her in a nursing home (not a great one) up north near Mom's new house. I rarely visited Grams then; only when I was in town to visit my mom and stepdad. Grams seemed cranky—mad at mom for putting her in the home. Perhaps she had a sense she was toward the end of life's journey. I knew her months in this world were numbered, and it was very difficult for me to see what the disease was beginning to do to my best friend.

On a Saturday evening in June 2006, Mom called and told me it was imperative that I drive up north the next day; the doctor didn't think Grammy would live more than a few days. This came as somewhat of a surprise for me. As I made the silent three-hour drive alone on Sunday, I was flooded with childhood memories and was curious and scared to see what state Grams was in at this point. I gathered my nerves of steel as best I could, mentally preparing myself. I arrived at Mom and Wayne's house, and then we drove over to the nursing home in two vehicles.

Mom didn't really prepare me for what to expect. Grams lay in her bed quietly moaning in pain, thinner than I'd ever seen her, dehydrated, pale, and not very coherent because of the morphine drops. I wanted to curl up in bed with her and hold her, but not if it hurt to even have someone touch her skin (which it would have—she still had remnants of the shingles she'd battled). I stood at the end of her bed with my stepdad, watching my mom give her ice chips. Somehow, Grams became conscious enough to recognize that I was standing there, and I told her I loved her, to which she returned the sentiment and added, "Such a pretty girl."

That was it. I was ready to burst into tears, and I didn't want to upset Grams by doing so, so I indicated to Wayne that I needed to go back to the house. He understood and quietly drove me home. After we arrived, I laid spread-eagle in the fresh and lush backyard grass, face toward the blue summer sky and warm sun, thinking, *I have just seen the face of death. I felt the cloak of it in her room. It's ready and waiting to take her.* It was a creepy feeling, otherworldly. I knew that day was the last time I would see her alive. I didn't hug or kiss Grams goodbye.

She hung on for five more days, until my aunt and uncle drove from Iowa to come see her. She passed away while I was taking a test in my college American history class on a Thursday evening. My mom called me after class to notify me. After hanging up, I melted onto the kitchen floor and sobbed. The viewing and funeral would be a combination one-day deal, since most of Gram's friends had already passed, and we had such a small family and list of friends.

Because the services were held at the Presbyterian church, an open coffin in the sanctuary was not permitted because of some silly old Scottish rule. I was irate that I couldn't view her as the pastor spoke the eulogy. I was ready to have a word with the pastor, but my mom and Matt held me back, saying there was nothing I could do. I sat in the front row of the sanctuary, sobbing uncontrollably during the entire service, with extended family behind me. My heart and body ached in places I didn't know they could. She was buried next to my grandfather in a local cemetery that had several of her family members already there.

Years later, I still think of her almost every day. Grammy played such an integral role in my childhood, and I have so many memories of her. She is a part of me. Luckily, I can still recall her voice and smell, her soft skin and pillowy hugs, her white fuzzy permed hair, red nail polish, and wrinkly hands. I remember such things now without a piercing pain through my heart. I had a very difficult time coping with her death for months afterward. I saw a grief counselor, and she assigned me the task of writing Grams a letter: I could say whatever I wanted in it. Oddly enough, this was quite therapeutic for me and was the first step toward healing the grieving process. I still have the letter, tucked far away . . .somewhere.

I can't think of my stepdad Wayne without thinking of Brad Paisley. Well, a song by Brad Paisley: "He Didn't Have to Be."

Wayne came into my life when I was a senior in high school. He and my mom met through a Christian dating service. He didn't have any kids from his previous marriage. I recall after their first date, Mom and I were discussing the evening, she telling me how it went. I just had this gut feeling and told her that I thought she was supposed to be with him. Mom and Wayne went on another few dates before he came over and I actually met him. We ordered pizza, talked, and maybe played cards or something. Usually I *loathed* Mom's boyfriends, but Wayne and I just clicked. He was easy to talk to, he had a wry sense of humor (unlike my mom), and his nickname of "Bubba" was born that night, along with some other inside jokes.

He was a very generous person. He bought tickets for the three of us to attend the US Nationals figure-skating championships being held in Detroit that winter. I was so excited! He included me on some of their dinners out, which was nice. My mom became unemployed, and he helped her pay the rent for a few months until the lease was up. He worked at GM in Flint his entire career, after graduating from Cedarville College in Ohio.

Their wedding was held shortly after my high-school graduation, at a small country church with a few witnesses. Mom was moving into his house, and I was going to move in with an older girlfriend I knew from church. Wayne cosigned the loan of $2,500 for my first car; he didn't have to do that. He had good credit, I had none, and my mom's was always poor. Grateful and humbled by his kindness, I was never late on one payment.

After I married, my husband and I would drive up north to my mom and Wayne's retirement home several weekends a year, and of course Christmas was one of them. Wayne loved to eat; he was always so happy with the delicious goodies my mom had been making for days. The four of us would play cards, dominoes, or other games after dinner, laughing hard and often. Wayne laughed like I imagined Santa Claus would: his whole upper body jiggled a little, and he turned red in the face. There are memories of going out on his pontoon and cruising around the nearby lake in the summer. One winter, it was so frigid that the same lake froze solid, and Wayne and I went ice skating. What a hoot that was! He was like a little kid! When he tried out snowmobiling, Matt and I got to drive his fun new machines. But after Wayne took a spill and cracked some ribs on a daylong trip with friends, my mom made him sell them.

They decided to move to Florida one spring, rather on a whim. They had talked about being snowbirds and renting a place for a few months, but one night mom called me at home and informed me of their decision. I was extremely upset, but I kept most of it inside; they were set on moving, and no matter what I said, I would not change their minds. I clammed up for weeks. Matt and I flew down and spent

Christmas with them and got to see Wayne dressed up in a tux for their church's big Christmas concert. He looked like a proud chubby penguin. He was in the choir and also on the maintenance crew there. He loved helping at church (any one that he attended) in whatever way he could. He was a big-hearted, kind, giving, Christian man.

After a few years, they decided to move back to northern Michigan, promising they would see us and their friends more often. In reality: not so much. My mom has MS, and when she has painful flare-ups, she is a regular witch. (Well, she could be anyway, but the MS made her especially intolerable.) I was used to her verbal attacks from childhood, but Wayne was rather new to them. She would lash out and make us all miserable. Matt and I came to dread trips to visit them and went less frequently. Eventually Wayne wised up to Mom's wicked ways, and he and I spoke freely about how horrible she could be and make you not want to be around her. After that, on a few occasions, I would call her out on her crankiness and tell her to back off of Wayne. She responded that we were teaming up against her. Classic narcissist.

In early 2009, around the time Matt was in the hospital with his medical emergency (more on that in the next chapter), there were visible changes in Wayne. Mom drove downstate as often as she could to be with me, and Wayne came with her a time or two. He hardly talked, wandered the halls of the floor Matt was on, and just stood at the doorway to Matt's room, staring inside. His hands were a little shaky. In the waiting room, he told me that he and Mom were over—which I took with a grain of salt, not knowing what was up with him. That summer, my mom took him to two doctors, and he was diagnosed with acute frontal-lobe dementia. His life expectancy was less than three years.

Slowly, Wayne slipped away. The kind, gentle, generous soul became obstinate, belligerent, and at times physically violent. He experienced weird dreams, and his brain translated them to reality. After a domestic disturbance in which the police were called, Mom decided that Wayne was no longer safe to be around. The nursing-home aides came to pick him up, and he didn't seem to mind. But once he was in the home, he was very mad at Mom and would glare at her and not talk when she visited him. This went on for a few months.

His speech went first, and everything snowballed from there. Hints of the inside jokes he and I shared would sometimes surface during a visit. I sat next to him on his bed trying to make him chuckle, or sometimes he would point to something (like new shoes or a new purse) and I knew he realized he hadn't seen the item before, and so I told him about the item(s). He walked the halls aimlessly and wore a monitoring bracelet that would trigger the door alarm if he tried to go outside unsupervised. In time, he lost muscle mass and control of his bladder and bowels. His ability to swallow became an issue. He wore bibs at communal meals, where he was fed by one of the nurse assistants. Watching at close proximity as my beloved stepdad reverted to a dependent child was emotionally challenging.

The last time I saw Wayne alive was on Father's Day 2011. Matt and I drove to the nursing home and brought a Father's Day card to put on his bulletin board. It's always so sad when patients don't have anything on their board—at least my mom made sure Wayne always had pictures and cards displayed. We sat for a short time in his room, and he seemed very vacant. Lunch was called, and he was taken via wheelchair (his leg muscles were atrophying) to the dining room. We followed him there and realized this could very well be a last good-bye.

Matt leaned down and hugged Wayne first, saying "I love you" and "I hope to see you on the other side someday" as his eyes watered. I choked up hearing that, but hiding my tears, I took my turn to hug my Bubba. I forced a smile, touched his short coarse grey hair, and told him he had been a great dad to me and that I loved him very much. I lived suspended in those few seconds so I could have a lingering memory of the last embrace from a feeble man who used to give me big bear hugs.

Matt and I started toward the door to exit the dining room, and then we turned around to look at Wayne one last time. He was watching us walk away and waved, smiling like an innocent child. From the hallway, we waved avidly back with smiles pasted on our faces. This was good-bye. I cried on the drive home.

The day he passed, a few months later, my mom called us in a panic and told us to hurry over to the nursing home—hospice had said Wayne was rapidly declining. We hurried over to meet Mom there, but he was already gone. His hospice nurse had been there holding his hand when it happened, so he wasn't alone. I don't think I could have handled it if I'd had to watch him pass, so in a way it was a relief. He was laid out straight and proper in his bed, covered with just a sheet. His eyes were closed.

Usually creeped out by touching the deceased, I sat on the edge of his bed and calmly touched Wayne's hairy forearm (which was still warm) and rubbed the short stubble on his head. I could see through the sheet his gut cavity was sunken in—that's how thin he had gotten. I could see and feel his ribs through the sheet. The three of us took our turn sitting and saying good-bye before taking a difficult leave. My mom spent the night at our house so she wasn't alone in her grief. We had a bonfire, since Wayne liked camping, to celebrate his life; we roasted marshmallows and then each of us wrote a note to Wayne on a piece of paper. We tossed our letters into the fire and the embers floated heavenward, carrying our messages with them.

Wayne's funeral was small and simple. My mom chose not to have him embalmed or to have a viewing, so there was only a graveside service a few days later. I brought a dozen blue and yellow helium-filled balloons—University of Michigan team colors, since he was a hardcore fan—with me to the cemetery. After the pastor read some Bible verses and a depressing death poem, I unfurled the balloons, fighting the gusty wind to do so, and released them one at a time, symbolizing his spirit letting go of this earth. Our small group of friends and family thought it was the perfect touch and that Wayne would have loved it.

A month or so later, my mom held a memorial service at their church up north, which friends and several church members attended. Uncle Kyle and Aunt Rita drove over from Traverse City. Matt and I drove from downstate; we were each to say something about Wayne before the pastor spoke. My mom had prepared some picture boards, and they stood near the entrance to the sanctuary. As the four of us waited in the front row for the service to begin, Mom flitted around the church, laughing, being a social butterfly, and making me sick to my stomach. She did not look to be mourning *at all.* It seemed plain disrespectful to me.

The memorial started with the normal hymns and recited prayers. A few people spoke, and the amiable pastor did a pleasant job of honoring Wayne's memory in a casual manner, which was fitting. The chubby boy from West Virginia from then on would be just a memory, but a very fond and special one for me.

After the service, there was the traditional church luncheon in the dining hall, which was too loud for the occasion, if you ask me. Again, my mother overplayed her role, more like hostess than bereaved. I wanted to throw some cheesy potatoes at her face and handcuff her to a cheap plastic chair. I couldn't wait to leave and be alone to process the day's events and the feelings they caused within me.

In September 2012, I participated in a local Walk to End Alzheimer's event. It was almost a year to the day since Wayne's passing. I had to raise some funds to participate in the event. After checking in, I was given a memory flower and T-shirt. The course was peaceful—a nature trail that ironically encircled my grandma's hospital of choice. As I enjoyed the early fall day, I was pensive as memories surfaced of

Grammy and Wayne. Wayne also lost his mother to the disease, so I thought of her, too. I had written all three of their names on my turquoise memory flower.

A solemn period gave way to one of appreciation and gratefulness. Rather than dwell on the sad passing of my loved ones, I began to become aware of how fortunate I was to have them as my family. One has no say about the family he or she is born into, but I was so lucky that Marge was the best grandmother I could have asked for. And although Wayne didn't come into my life until I was seventeen, the twenty years I was privileged to be his daughter (he never referred to me as his stepdaughter) brought some of the highlights of my life. I lifted my face toward the sunny sky and smiled.

Chapter 5

Which Way is Up?

When I went to bed at twelve thirty in the morning on March 18, 2009, I had absolutely no clue that my life was about to be turned upside down. A phone ringing at two in the morning is never good, especially when the ICU at the local hospital is on the other end of the phone telling me to rush my butt over because my husband was just admitted to that floor.

The previous week, Matt had spent five days at that hospital, suffering from extreme stomach cramping, bloating in the gut, and difficulty passing bowel movements. Three different doctors were assigned to his case. Several tests were run to pinpoint the cause of his discomfort. Matt was put on a liquid-only diet and then gradually reintroduced to solid food. He was discharged within five days with instructions to contact the discharge/lead doctor to schedule another test the following week.

Matt had a very hard time sleeping and eating, and he generally felt like crap for the next two days. By midday Tuesday, the pain became intolerable, and his mom drove him back to the same hospital's ER. I was working at a local government agency at the time; in fact, I recall it was St. Patrick's Day because I wore a green shirt to work. Matt's sister Debbie called me on my direct desk-phone line around noon and told me very calmly that I needed to leave work and go the emergency room ASAP. Something inside me knew she was putting on a calm front, and I was therefore dreading going back to the hospital. I tidied my cubicle, organized case files and paperwork, and labeled what piles of folders were with Post-It notes. Then I left for "lunch," not knowing when or if I would return.

The scene I encountered as I entered the ER was intimidating. Our former pastor and his wife (a semi-retired nurse), who are also Matt's cousins, met me near the entry. Anna was there, as she had driven Matt over. He was in one of the curtained bays in the otherwise open ER. He was hooked up to a vitals machine and his skin was grey—it looked like Tim Burton had stopped by to give him a bad Hollywood makeup job. Matt's eyes were wide, crazed, and scared out of pain and confusion. He was almost hyperventilating.

I sure didn't know what the heck was going on, what the numbers on the monitor meant, why nurses were giving him meds, or what the drugs were for. I was alone in a room full of people. You know how in movies, they record a scene and it looks like you're viewing it through a tunnel? That's what it was like for me to experience this chaotic environment. Our cousin repeatedly went to the nurse's station and demanded a doctor admit Matt and run certain tests. Her tone told me this was *very* serious, as she is normally a gentle lamb of a woman.

Someone came to take Matt for a CAT scan. The fear in his eyes as they wheeled him off made me feel helpless. Shortly upon his return, a male nurse inserted a catheter because Matt felt as if he had to pee but couldn't. Hopefully he would be able to produce something without thinking about it with the catheter in. After several hours of pacing, panicking, and feeling ignored and helpless, we learned Matt had been finally and formally readmitted by the doctor who had discharged him just a few days earlier, and he would be sent up to the same general medical floor he had been on the previous week. In fact, it was the same room, same bed number. Not a good omen.

It was eight at night before Matt was finally settled into his room. A college-student nurse-in-training would be looking after him for the night shift. He was not connected to a monitor or oxygen. He was thirstier than a camel. He was on pain medicine by this time, though I don't know the name of it or the dosage. We mindlessly watched *American Idol* on TV. The student eventually cut off his water supply, thinking it was probably not normal to consume as much as he was (it wasn't).

The doctor came to his room around ten, said he was surprised to see Matt back at the hospital, and offered surgery that evening or the next day. I can't clearly recall if he specified a diagnosis or what the surgery would be for. They agreed to do surgery the following day. I stayed with Matt until about ten thirty, when I could tell he was sleepy and would probably drift off within minutes of my departure. He needed rest after such a crazy day.

When I arrived home, I felt guilty that Cooper, our yellow Labrador, had missed dinner and no one had been there to let him outside. I took care of the dog, and then a nesting sensation kicked in. I did laundry, ran the dishwasher, cleaned the house, you name it. That had only happened to me once before—the night my father-in-law passed away of cancer at his home under hospice care. After two hours, I was finally tired enough to retire. It was twelve thirty when I went to bed.

When the phone rang at two in the morning, it scared the crap out of me. I couldn't think straight; my brain was a hurricane of swirling thoughts as I wondered what the heck had happened in the last few hours that could possibly cause Matt to end up in the ICU. I hurriedly threw on a burgundy velour track suit and called Anna—no doubt scaring the crap out of her as well—and then sprinted out of my house and drove like crazy. Fortunately, we lived only ten minutes from the hospital at the time. But of course I got every red light when there was not a soul on the roads except for me. I *so* wanted to run them all. I'm sure I violated some speed laws in the quick yet endless-seeming drive.

As I was waiting to turn left onto the road where the hospital was located, as scrambled as my brain was, I distinctly felt a fleeting calm, along with the words, *Don't worry—it'll be okay.* As a Christian, I knew God's spirit was reaching out to help calm me. After a few seconds, however, I shook my head as if to erase the fuzziness and said to the empty car, "What? Not worry? *What's* going to be okay?!"

I pulled into the hospital drive and parked in the ER parking lot because that was the only entrance open at such an ungodly hour. I followed the maze of hallways, watching for directional signs to the main elevators. I broke into a flat-out run, weaving my way through the dark and eerily quiet hallways. Again, it felt like a scene from a movie. I even remember thinking that as I was sprinting through the hospital. I wondered how many hidden cameras caught me running through the darkness like a madwoman.

I reached the eighth floor where all the ICU rooms plus two nurse's stations were located, and as I proceeded forward down the hallway to the patient rooms, I had a bad feeling that the one lit up with several nurses running in and out in a panic was Matt's. What was I about to see? How bad could he be? Fear made me want to stop in my tracks, but I knew that wasn't an option.

As much as I didn't want to keep walking, that's what I did. I cautiously and anxiously stepped just inside the first room on the left, room 821, the site of the activity. What I saw almost made me faint.

Matt was barely conscious and had returned to the pasty grey color from earlier in the day. Several nurses were calling out orders, asking questions, buzzing in and out of his room, adding bags to the IV drip poles, pushing meds into tubes, and not telling me anything. I seemed in their way, so I stood aside, staring in confused awe at the state Matt was in. So many questions, thoughts, and feelings ran through my mind and heart as I watched the action.

Thankfully, within ten minutes, Anna arrived with our cousin/pastor, the same one from the previous day. At least we could be confused and worry together as a unit. Soon after that, the doctor appeared—the same one who had discharged Matt on Sunday and visited him just hours before. He performed a quick analysis of Matt and the situation, and then he proceeded to the nurse's station to make several phone calls. I heard him raise his voice in a forceful manner to whoever he was talking to. *This is very serious*, I silently realized.

When the doctor returned, I demanded to know what was going on. He didn't tell me everything, only that he had to call a surgical team in because my husband needed emergency surgery *now*. The gravity of that statement fell heavily on me. Did this mean that Matt could possibly die?

As I stood by Matt's bedside, holding his hand amidst the chaos, a pre-op nurse started asking me tons of questions, and I lost my patience. I raised my voice over all the talking and my husband's potentially dying body and told her to *back off*. This was a lot for me to process, and these were possibly the last moments I would have with him. She stepped back and left me alone. I hadn't gotten a Q&A with anyone, didn't know what was going on, and she was grilling *me* for answers that should be in his chart? *I don't think so!* I would later feel bad about how I treated her; she was just doing her job, as they say. But what about the human side? What about showing some compassion instead of collecting data from someone on the verge of a meltdown?

Several nurses and the doctor suggested Anna and I say good-bye (for now? forever?) before Matt was taken to the OR. Was he dying in front of us? We wept and prayed, and our pastor did too. We held Matt's hands, since he already had tubes all over the place, ready for surgery. We were then instructed to go to the surgical waiting room. More dark, eerie mazes through the labyrinth of hallways on the ground floor to the complete other side of the hospital.

The waiting room was huge, dark, quiet, and cold, with lots of windows. I chose a loveseat to lie on and then let my emotions go. Hysterical, hyperventilating, nonstop crying ensued. Anna was dealing with her own grief, pain, and questions, so our cousin attempted to console both of us—more me, since I was visibly falling apart. He said reassuring things, quoted Bible verses, and prayed. He rubbed my back, hugged and held me, and acted like a father.

The nurse I'd lashed out at suddenly reappeared and apologized for the earlier scene, brought me some blankets since I was shivering (due to nerves, mostly), and conveyed that she discovered we were Christians, so it was in Jesus's hands. No kidding. She meant well, but I wanted to be left alone.

That's not entirely true—I needed my family, but it wasn't even four in the morning. We waited to call family members until around five thirty. I called my mom, dad, and Matt's nephew Mark, who lived in Traverse City and would have a torturous four-hour drive ahead of him. Anna and our cousin called people on their cell phones too. I just hoped that if Matt didn't die in surgery, family would arrive in time in case he didn't hold on very long afterward.

The three-hour surgery was a never-ending purgatory. So many thoughts and feelings overwhelmed me. I kept telling our cousin I felt I hadn't been a good-enough wife. We hadn't tried hard enough with our relationship. Matt and I had struggled with many issues during our marriage. Some days, it seemed a battle just to stay together. If he died, would I still be considered a Bowen? I didn't want to be a widow. What if Matt was on the OR table right then, innards all over the place, flatlining? Any second Matt could potentially die, and I wouldn't have the chance to speak from my overly emotional heart to him.

The doctor finally came out to the waiting room, called the three of us into a small consulting room, and closed the door. The room was painted orange and dimly lit. I sat on the floor straight across from the doctor, a coffee table between us. He discussed the procedure he'd performed, but I only heard and understood about half of the information he was sharing. I asked him to draw a diagram of what he did to my husband's body. I could tell he thought it was an odd request, but I didn't care—I wanted a visual so I could understand it better.

When the surgeon opened Matt's abdominal cavity, he found it full of feces. A portion of Matt's small intestine had become blocked, and the tissue slowly died – hence the pain he suffered the previous week. Toxins and pressure built up and the intestine eventually perforated in three spots. The doctor removed the dead tissue and reconnected Matt's intestine together. Although he sutured the layers of abdominal muscles together, the doctor left the large vertical incision open, so as to allow quick and easy access should Matt need to go back in for another procedure.

I would later learn bits of what happened after I left the hospital the evening before. Apparently, Matt had drifted in and out of sleep. He felt like he had to make a bowel movement, so he got himself out of bed and began to walk toward his bathroom. He felt dizzy, blacked out, and collapsed onto the hard floor.

We never did discover the length of time that passed before he was attended to by nursing staff. We do know a Code Blue was issued over the hospital loudspeaker, and the Blue Crew came from ICU to Matt's room to resuscitate him. He was not responsive. The nurses did CPR for several minutes and cracked a few ribs before he came to. He was taken immediately to the eighth floor.

The pain Matt had been in for a week was the blocked bowel tissue actually dying, and when he got up from his hospital bed, the small intestine ruptured, sending him into septic shock, cardiac arrest, and liver, kidney, and respiratory failure.

Even though the surgery was successful, the chances of Matt pulling through were very slim. Family started to arrive in the surgical waiting room, including Debbie and Matt's nephew Daryl*. By the time the small group of us reached room 821, our cousin David was already waiting in Matt's room. I was surprised but relieved to see him; he and Matt were best friends growing up, and supposedly got into legendary trouble on occasion.

Matt was in such critical condition post-op that he had his very own nurse all day, a one-to-one ratio. That only happens when situations are *very* serious. (Of course, I wasn't aware of this at the time; I had yet to receive the medical crash course I was about to get.) The nurse was very focused, kind, and willing to explain things to me. I could ask her questions, but she was careful how she answered some of them. She was very busy charting and checking all day. Matt had eleven IV bags flowing into various lines and ports. He was hooked to a heart rate/pulse/oxygen monitor. The meaning of the numbers was still foreign to me.

As the day progressed, more family and close friends came. No one could believe it. When my mom and Mark finally showed up, they had to lift my dead weight of 135 pounds off the hallway floor after I crumbled down to it when the nurse told me it was not a good idea for me to quickly run home to take a shower. That's how bad Matt was—they wanted next of kin available in the ICU. I could not walk; I could barely stand.

From this point forward, I must admit that timing and events and people get somewhat fuzzy. There was so much I had to attend to; my mind was in ten places at once, 24/7, for three months. People commented later that I should have kept a journal to note and remember everything that happened and when. I didn't. Sure, it would have come in handy for the medical malpractice lawsuit we filed, and for writing this story, but looking back, it's been hard enough to move forward with life, and I'm glad I don't have such a personal and intimate memento hanging around. It's in the past, and it needs to stay there.

I do recall this: Matt's oxygen levels were in the low seventies on Saturday and Sunday (normal is anywhere in the upper nineties), so he was placed in a drug-induced coma and hooked up to a ventilator so more oxygen could be forced into his lungs without making him uncomfortable. Because of the renal failure, his body weight swelled by over a hundred pounds of pure liquid. Sunday there was a crash cart in the hallway outside his room; the staff thought he would die that day for sure. In the waiting room, I sobbed on my dad's University of Michigan sweatshirt, crying, "I don't want to be a widow. I'm not ready for this."

People from church, more family, and close friends began to arrive, nearly all at once. Somehow word had gotten out to the masses that Matt was dying. I was touched to see how many people came to be with me, Anna, and Debbie on that awful day. As I've mentioned, we are Christians, and let me tell you: the group of fifty or so of us present had ourselves a *prayer meetin'* right there in that waiting room, which was adjacent to Matt's room. Some people went to the wall dividing the two rooms and put their hands on it and prayed and cried. It literally became a wailing wall. I was in a recliner the nurses brought in specifically for my comfort, covered in blankets, shivering, holding hands with this circle of love, faith, and determination, and if ever my spirit wailed, from a place way down deep I didn't know existed, it did that day.

Matt was placed on dialysis that evening—a tricky move, since he was retaining fluid and had gained excessive fluid weight in three days, which was putting pressure on his lungs and heart. He was in such a fragile state, some doctors were fearful his weakened body wouldn't tolerate the procedure. It was a shot in the dark.

No matter the state of our marriage, Matt was the closest person in the world to me, and I was going to fight with all I had, since he couldn't. We all left the ICU that night with Matt still alive, but I was fearful of receiving another nighttime phone call. My friend Rachel came to stay with me and take care of Cooper or run errands. She slept with me those first few scary nights so I didn't feel alone.

Monday morning, Daryl was already at the hospital when I arrived. He had brought me McDonald's for breakfast and left it on the table in the waiting room. He wasn't in there, so I walked into Matt's room. Daryl was standing just looking at Matt and the monitor. The numbers were so much improved over Sunday's!

I asked, "Are those for real? Is it true?"

He said "Yeah" with a smile and put his arm around my shoulder. Maybe this was the upturn we had prayed for.

In the coming weeks and months, I transformed from a shy, conflict-avoiding mouse of a girl to a lady to be reckoned with. I memorized the names of Matt's meds, what their function was, and how often he needed them. I was on a first-name basis with all the ICU nurses, even the floor supervisor. Matt had approximately nine doctors popping in every day (one nurse wrote down their specialties and names for me, bless her soul) to look at his chart and check on him. I tried not to leave his room, or if I did, I told the nurses where I was so I could speak with a doctor before he or she scurried off. And if the doc did scurry off, I had the nurses page him to return to the ICU. I wanted, needed, and deserved to be kept informed. I became the Patient Advocate from Hell. I was no doubt annoying to some doctors and nurses, but most of them I got along just fine with, and they seemed to respect my vigilance for excellent care.

Apparently, Matt had a heart attack when he "coded" on the general medical floor, so a cardiologist was assigned to him. He was septic, so an infectious-disease doctor checked on him every day and adjusted his antibiotics as needed. The kidney specialist was an old, tall, grumpy coot who, no matter how nice I was, never cracked a smile. Getting information out of him was like pulling teeth. I liked the respiratory doctor and nurses; they were frank and friendly. And they were as determined as I was about weaning Matt off the ventilator once he came out of the drug-induced coma, transferring him to a tracheotomy, and eventually getting him off of that as well. The dialysis team consisted of several very nice men; sometimes we chatted, sometimes they sat quietly as I slept in the recliner in Matt's room, by now my second home. Usually Matt needed an Ativan to relax, since for some reason his blood pressure would always rise during the four- to five-hour blood-purification cycle. A doctor from the physical-therapy floor paid a visit and then decided Matt wouldn't fit into the tight guidelines of the PT program.

Once the extra water weight had been removed through dialysis, which took a few weeks, and Matt's kidneys started to function once again (thank you Jesus!), he looked very thin, gaunt, and pale. He was on a bed with a scale, but it didn't seem reliable. I spoke with the main doctor and his associate about what kind of nourishment he was receiving from the TPN bag—a white liquid substance on an IV drip that needed changing every twelve hours. The TPN drip had just enough of everything needed to keep a person from dying, but nothing to aid in recovery or supply nutrients. I demanded a consultation with a dietician about jacking his TPN contents up several notches to include more calcium, protein, and iron, especially since he was (and always will be) a bariatric patient with less absorption capability than the average person. The dietician definitely saw the need and made her recommendations to the kidney doctor. He agreed Matt's body could handle the content increase and signed the order.

There developed a pattern to my days at the hospital. Get up by seven thirty, feed the pets, shower, drive to the hospital, and get a donut and coffee on the way up to the eighth floor. If Matt was asleep, I didn't wake him. I just sat in the recliner in the dark of his ICU room and read or did word puzzles. Sometimes I would camp out in the waiting room (not once turning the TV on) and use the Clorox wipes I brought every day in my canvas bag to wipe down the entire room and bathroom. All the cleaning attendants did at night was empty the trash; that's simply not good enough in ICU!

Family straggled in and out throughout the days, helping to pass the time. Some even brought me lunch or a small gift. A few were "regulars," those who were very close to our family: David, his sister Carmen, Matt's friend Chad, and Rodger, yet another cousin. When we were all in the waiting room together, we would talk about Matt as if we were huddled around a campfire sharing old family tales. It was kind of nice talking about him, and he had no way to defend himself! Lighter moments like those gave me strength, which I needed. The hardest thing for me to do was to ask for help, admit I was in need, and be vulnerable; but my boss at the time told me that people can't be blessed for helping if I don't let them. There was a full circle to this.

I knew approximately when the specific doctors came to check on Matt, so I timed my lunch and afternoon around their schedule. Sometimes it was nice just being alone up there, either in the waiting room or in room 821. I was spending twelve hours each day at the hospital with no breaks. By the time nine o'clock came and I knew who Matt's night-shift nurse was and saw that he got his first dose of nighttime meds, I was relieved to pack up my bag, put my puffy winter coat on, and take the elevator downstairs. The chilly nighttime air both revitalized me and made me realize how drained I was. Often one of our male cousins would escort Anna and me outside to the dark, nearly vacant parking lot.

In the middle of all of the above chaos, one of the drugs Matt was placed on post-op, Levophed, was drawing blood away from extremities and toward the torso or vital organs. The unfortunate side effect of this medication was poor circulation in the hands and feet. Matt's hands were slowly turning lavender. His feet were becoming blotchy, with colors including raspberry, purple, and dark pink. I kept questioning the nurses and doctors about what was happening and what the plan of action was. They were rather tight-lipped in regard to the latter. Finally, Matt's main doctor/surgeon told me that he had seen this before: it happened all the time when he worked at another hospital. The toes eventually die, shrivel up, and fall off. Yes, you read that right. A twenty-first-century doctor was going to allow a medieval process to take place on my husband. *Um, I don't think so.*

Our nurse cousin and Daryl said I had a legal right to request a consultation with a specifically named specialist. Within twenty-four hours, the lead doctor would have to sign off on my request and approve the consultation, and the new doctor would have to visit Matt. At that point in the game, I wasn't messing around. Daryl gave me the name of an orthopedic surgeon who was highly regarded among his peers, and that's the name I wrote on my consult request. Guess who showed up the next day?

The orthopedic doctor thoroughly inspected Matt's toes and feet, instructing the nurse how to dress them correctly. He said surgery would be necessary to amputate all ten toes because Matt had developed gangrene. I kind of figured that would be his determination, but it was still not easy news to hear. He was a kind and sympathetic doctor with good bedside manner, and I immediately felt I could trust him. He would schedule the procedure for the following week. In the meantime, Matt's toes became black, cold, shriveled raisins, and the pain level in his feet continued to climb. Supposedly it was because of the dying tissue. Months later, we would realize it was neuropathy (a painful nerve condition) setting in.

Occupational and physical therapy were prescribed, though mostly it was physical therapy, done in Matt's hospital bed. I liked the young man in charge of Matt's case. He was a person of few words but something about him made me feel comfortable. So one afternoon around three thirty, when two female physical therapists came rushing into Matt's room to do therapy after he'd already had dialysis for five hours and was dog-tired, you can imagine my surprise and dissatisfaction. They were loud, flipped on the bright room lights, and were talking about how they couldn't wait to be done with their shift at four. Matt was immediately confused and panicked; he figured at that point in the day, he wouldn't have therapy.

As the gals began to do therapy with Matt, his heart rate kept rising, and I did not want them to continue, especially since they were in such a hurry to speed through their last patient of the day and go home. I got Matt's assigned nurse and demanded the therapy department supervisor take a meeting with me—*now.* Then I proceeded to chew out the physical therapists about the way they were treating their patient, my husband. They left at my request, and within minutes I was sitting in the waiting room with their boss (who was younger than me). I informed her that Matt would *not* be treated like that in the future by her staff. I never saw any of them again, only the quiet man.

The day of the amputation, Matt was in fairly good spirits when the anesthesiologist came to take him to the operating room. I sat in the same waiting room as I had over a month before, this time not worried about whether he would die but how life would be for him, and us, with this change. Several family members were present, among them Anna, Debbie, devoted cousin David, our former pastor and his wife, Matt's uncle, and a few others.

I felt so guilty about something, and I felt I had to confess it to our cousin. I pulled her aside from the group and told her that, in the past, when Matt and I would watch TV in the evening from our recliners, I would look at his toes and think, *Man, those long toes are ug-ly!* We laughed, and I felt bad but relieved at the same time. I almost felt like just thinking that thought in the past contributed to this current situation. Of course it didn't, but it bothered me nonetheless.

Matt was in such pain that night he actually begged me to stay and not go home. How could I say no to that? As much as I desired my own warm comfy bed and escape from the hospital for twelve hours, I resigned myself to the fact that it was something I had to do. Years later, he would tell me he never remembered that night or the fact that he asked me to stay. Dilaudid will do that to a person.

Neither of us really slept. The night nurse was kind enough to check on us and brought me juice and crackers, since I'd had no dinner and little appetite. I had brought Matt some squeeze stress balls to use for some occupational therapy, but that evening, he squeezed them out of pain. I sat vigilant all night, watching the agony cross his face and make him moan. Debbie arrived to relieve me the next morning so I could go home and take a nap for a few hours. By then, I was ready to be put in my own drug-induced coma! The orthopedic surgeon came and recast Matt's feet two days after surgery. The suture line was quite good and ended up healing nicely.

Since the physical therapy unit couldn't accept him as a patient (he had to be weight-bearing, and he couldn't be for six weeks), Matt was discharged from the hospital one week after the amputation. In that short timespan, Matt's nurse cousin and I had toured local nursing homes, choosing the one with the biggest and most comprehensive physical- and occupational-therapy rooms and programs. You have no idea how hard it is to pick a nursing home for your forty-four-year-old husband, praying to God he won't be there permanently. At times, the thought was too overwhelming for me.

The home accepted Matt as a patient, and the hospital social worker had a lot to do in just a few days' time. So did the nursing staff. Matt had to be transferred from IV pain meds to oral pain meds; his trach hole was slowly healing; and there was still the open abdominal wound that the doctor said would close itself naturally but would need special attention by someone trained in wound care. (At this point in the game, I was trained in that and *so* much more.) The male physical therapist worked Matt's leg muscles while he was in bed that last week, since Matt couldn't stand.

Before he left the ICU, Matt had some new visitors: people who had been too scared to come early on when things were bad. His day nurse those last few days was one of our favorites, and she gave us some tips for the transition to a nursing-home environment, since she used to work at one. Any and all supplies that had been brought into Matt's room—bandages, creams, gauze, tape—were ours for the taking. Every evening, I took home a stash of something. And thank God I did, because the nursing home had no clue how to dress a wound as large as Matt's. It would take days to receive supplies that I had at home only twenty minutes away.

Matt could have died on several occasions, save for the Lord's divine intervention. I myself was a somewhat confused Christian at the time. Matt has been steadfast his entire life. It's unfathomable how Christ "decides" who to bestow miracles upon; it's one of life's mysteries. Matt could have been brain-damaged or brain-dead because of lengthy periods of low oxygen. He could have died from the heart attack, respiratory failure, or kidney failure. His gangrene could have spread to his arms and legs, thus requiring more extreme amputation. He could have become addicted to the high amount of pain medication he was on. For a long time, I felt nothing but grateful and had nothing to complain about. My husband survived against all odds.

As I reported to my temporary job as Matt's advocate every day, I never entertained the notion that his heart, lungs, and kidneys would not recover. I wouldn't let his handicap stop him. From deep down in my soul, from the moment God spoke to my spirit in my car, I just forged ahead, not accepting anything less than complete recovery, seeking medical information I felt I was not being provided, stalking WebMD, and drawing from a strength I never knew I possessed. I know that God directed me as Matt's advocate, because I was *so* out of my element and did things I didn't know I was capable of.

The above description of "the Event" (as we now refer to it) is extremely condensed. For me to detail the seven-week stay at the nursing home that followed would require another lengthy chapter. In fact, the Event alone could fill its own book. I have omitted many details so as not to bore you with too much medical jargon and to stay sane while reliving this awful period with every typed word.

Today, Matt has orthopedic inserts/supports for his shoes. He cannot stand for long periods of time. A cane is always within reach. The neuropathy is ceaseless and unrelenting. No prescription drug relieves the severe pain he is constantly in. He uses the electrical-powered carts at grocery stores and malls. We have had to partially alter vacations to suit his limits. He can still drive—I can't imagine how—but he has a permanent handicapped window card. He suffered from drug withdrawal and depression for months. He had to leave his job and is now on SSI and Medicare.

It was hard for me to return to my demanding job after twelve weeks of FMLA leave. Matt was staying with his mom, who could watch him 24/7 when I couldn't. She also drove him to numerous doctor and therapy appointments since I couldn't take any more time off work. I went from being strong one week to an exhausted, supersensitive, confused mess the next as I plunged back into "normal life." That summer, I sought counseling and was diagnosed with posttraumatic stress disorder, anxiety, and depression. It took a while, but the right medicine at the right dosage got me through each day. However, something in my limbic system just wasn't recovering, and I saw three different therapists before I felt I was given some tools, mantras, and literature to help me get back to being more like my old self. My mental health slowly improved after I finally left my job and the toxic stress it caused.

In answer to the question posed by this chapter title—"Which way is up?"—I suppose my response would be this: Imagine diving in the ocean, and you get disoriented. Your oxygen tank is getting low. You know you need to make it to the surface. You look around for the point where the sun's rays are piercing through the water. Finding that spot, you change the pressure on your flotation unit and slowly float up toward the faint light. You can't go too fast, or you may get the bends. When the surface is breached, you are relieved, exhausted, and amazed at the fear you felt down below. Getting back into the boat, you rest, and with the help of your mates, you wrestle out of your gear and tight wetsuit and try to relax.

I conquered the power of the darkness. But I wasn't alone, and that's why I am still here.

Chapter 6

Dark Clouds

There they sit on the countertop: the five pills that I rely on every day to make me feel and act "normal." That is to say, not suicidal, agoraphobic, anxious, moody, or any derivative of those. I need the pills, yet I hate them. After Matt's near-death experience, once life calmed down a bit, my internist and my counselor detected symptoms of posttraumatic stress disorder (PTSD), anxiety, and depression.

As described in earlier chapters, I had a not-so-lovely childhood, and when I look back at it, I think perhaps I was depressed a bit back then because of my circumstances and the way I was treated by family and school staff. My narcissistic mother made me feel like an amoeba, my father tried his best to love me in the limited time increments he was given, and my stepmother made it clear she wished I wasn't alive. A crummy family life plus being shy, low-income, and not popular at school filled me with feelings of worthlessness early in life.

In the twenty or so years since high-school graduation, I continued to struggle with sadness. Not all of the time, but often. I definitely think I developed seasonal affective disorder, as winter became a dreaded Michigan condition to endure. My self-esteem grew in my years at community college; I not only earned an associate's degree, but learned what I was capable of as a person. Even with a full-time (stressful) job and part-time classes, I earned a 3.68 GPA.

During the three months Matt was under acute medical care, I was in constant fight-or-flight mode, and something I would come to know as hypervigilant. I was fighting for his life, his care, and his progress because he couldn't. When my twelve weeks of (unpaid) FMLA expired, I had to return to work immediately. No decompression time. No preparation time. I grudgingly walked into the rear of the office building that morning feeling like I used to on the first day of school: nervous, hesitant, and afraid of the unknown. My mind was elsewhere, wondering about Matt all day.

I became indifferent about many things in the office environment—things that seemed superficial, trivial, or petty. That medical experience changed the course of my life forever. At a time when I was just learning to be confident and comfortable with myself, this huge event occurred and knocked me off-course, drastically. The old Stacy was no more; I didn't know who the gal with PTSD was or if I even liked her.

It was a daily, hourly struggle to find balance within myself. I practiced yoga once a week with a pal from work. That helped some—having some "me" time, stretching my tense muscles, breathing out all the stress. I started running that summer and signed up for a 5K race in the fall at the local zoo. I was struggling to act professional and leave my personal life at home while at work, even though my personal life now *was* my life—period. I couldn't drop thoughts and feelings I endured because of the medical trauma at the office door at seven thirty in the morning and pick them back up at four in the afternoon.

I used to be decent at compartmentalizing my life, something men are more known for than women. But now, everything was thrown off balance. Different areas of my life came to be intertwined, and I felt caught in a dark, swirling cyclone, with problems, feelings, issues, and people circling around me, out of reach and control. I felt like an octopus being pulled in eight different directions. On occasion, in my lower moments, I indulged in alcohol, at times to excess. After I realized this made my migraines and depression worse, I no longer wanted to subject myself to the self-destructive behavior that ran on both sides of my family. On bad days I still struggle with the angel on one shoulder and the devil on the other.

Through counseling, I learned about "the new normal" that comes after a major life event. In my case, I had to learn not to compare things in the present with those pre-trauma. As much as I just wanted to turn off my brain and go dormant for a season, I had no choice but to move forward and learn about reconstructing my frame of mind and coping with unfamiliar feelings—an exhausting task after what I had been through. My hypervigilance was an automatic response to certain stimuli, and I had to consciously work on reducing that in order to let go of the incident so that Matt could relearn to rely on himself instead of me.

My friends, family, and fellow church members were awesome during the critical time when Anna, Matt, and I needed them the most. But as Matt improved, many fell away, or rather, went back to *their* normal life (I don't blame them). During recovery and physical therapy, I refused to let Matt feel sorry for himself, knowing that if I gave him the slightest indication it was okay to play the victim, he would give up and not press on. To some, my "tough love" approach might have seemed cold, but it was the only way for him to gain any independence. I told him (and myself) that the new normal—which included shoe prosthetics and using a scooter cart at stores or a cane at church—was no big deal.

Being strong for Matt weakened me considerably. The migraines I'd started experiencing at thirty became more frequent. I began to lose weight and interest in a regular eating schedule. The fight-or-flight behavior seeped into my attitude at work, causing me to be highly defensive and sensitive. My voiced opinions got me a few warnings.

My internist placed me on an anti-depressant and a medicine for anxiety. Those helped some, but considering most of my days were spent in a stressful work environment, I couldn't tell how much. He added a mood stabilizer to my regimen after a few months. I ended up taking short-term disability leave under the direction of my internist and my counselor, giving me some of the time I had needed a year prior to talk about my feelings, and allowing me to take my focus off of Matt and work through the residual issues from PTSD. I ended up leaving my job, which was both a blessing and a burden.

My day as a newly unemployed person started when I stirred around four in the morning to pee; usually I fell back asleep afterward. However, by doing so, I often woke up late morning, around ten, instantly depressed at the thought of what I could have accomplished in the preceding hours: a morning walk or run, coffee and breakfast, a shower and sitting down with my computer to write or apply for some jobs. With these mini-failures (as I viewed them) pushing down on me, I felt defeated and longed to just stay cocooned in bed. But I knew I would only feel worse by doing so.

I dragged myself from the oasis of my bed and took my pills first thing. Then I popped a multivitamin, since I didn't always consciously make good food choices and even skipped meals at times. Since food preparation was rather low on my list of ambitions, I rarely planned dinner. That, in turn, made me feel like a bad wife, thus adding more kindling to my failure fire.

After the multivitamin, I made a beeline for the Keurig machine to make coffee. As my mood lightened and I slowly came around/woke up/emerged from my coma, I would take a shower. On some days, that was a major accomplishment in and of itself. Even though I have only ever worn fairly light makeup, many days I didn't even bother with that. Other days (usually when meeting a friend or going out for dinner) I did put some on to look put together, which in turn made me feel put together. Ah, illusions . . .

By midday, I turned to my faithful friend, my laptop PC. Depending on my degree of depression or optimism, I either job-hunted or worked on my writing or other creative projects for a few hours. If it was nice out, I tried to make myself go outdoors; whether to pick weeds, play with our dog, or just roam our property. This shouldn't have been a difficult task, as I love nature and craved the warm feeling of sunshine on my skin. Yet if my Labrador didn't need to relieve himself, there were days I probably wouldn't have even opened the door, let alone gone outside.

I came to hate driving in major traffic. My house was located in a semi-woodsy area and I'd become accustomed to having space, so road congestion freaked me out. Perhaps this was why errands seemed a chore, even though a feeling of accomplishment followed a completed task. I love nutritious food but hated to grocery shop. There were days when the anxiety of getting ready and going out in public overwhelmed me, and I chose to stay inside. Other days I forced myself out and then was exhausted upon my return home.

As anyone unemployed or unemployable can tell you, it takes a toll on you mentally. My depression worsened, and I became very irritable and moody. The beginning was the worst. Every day I spent hours on the computer job-searching—*that* became my job. The isolation, constant research, and unfruitful searching and applying made me feel like a failure more often than not. I was not landing interviews. With an associate's degree and nearly twenty years of office experience, I couldn't understand why. I became a zombie, sleeping in, not changing out of my pajamas, and drinking coffee until mid-afternoon while networking and research/job surfing.

I was too wound up to go to bed at a normal hour and became a night owl. I was exhausted all of the time, though I wasn't really doing much. I had doctor and counselor appointments and might run an errand or two, but otherwise I was a hermit. It took everything in me to attend church on Sundays. To get showered and put on some jeans for a normal day at home was difficult enough; church required pantyhose and a smile. Some Sundays, I just couldn't face my fellow parishioners.

After service on a Sunday when I did attend, my cousin, who gives awesome hugs, came over and enveloped me. Not a quick grab and release, either. She *held* me. It was the first time I consciously felt my posture relax in months. She whispered in my ear and asked how I was doing, if I was okay. It dawned on me that I felt crappy and was not okay. I shared this revelation with her, whispering into her soft curly hair a simple "no." Then we cried. That was the first time I had said that aloud. I realized the mask I had been wearing had to disappear or I would.

Something released in me that day. I quit acting like I was okay, because I definitely wasn't. I had known this about myself, but until I honestly admitted it to my cousin, I'd suppressed it. The perma-smile came off. Even though Matt didn't die, he'd come dangerously close, and I had never grieved that. We were both missing parts of our previous selves. It was alright to grieve the loss of all that used to be and would never be again.

Once I accepted that, a certain amount of weight dropped from my shoulders. I stopped pretending. I let people see the hurt and told them things were different for me. I allowed myself to be vulnerable. No small feat for someone who'd spent most of her life with a wall around her heart.

I told people I was depressed and taking medication. In our society today and particularly in Christian communities—in my experience, at least—there is a stigma if one admits such a thing. I didn't want to be labeled crazy or nuts, or whatever negative names cruel people might associate with my condition. The people who mattered understood the underlying cause of my illness and were supportive. But I didn't want them to look at me with "sympathy eyes." I just wanted to be seen as Stacy, not the Miracle's Wife or the depressed lady. Just a woman evolving.

When I was attending community college, my adventurous side had emerged: I was interested in trying ethnic foods and exploring different parts of the metro Detroit area, and I couldn't get enough cultural exposure, from baseball games to the opera, musicals, and summer amphitheater concerts. After the physical and mental drama of Matt's illness, it was difficult for my friends and family to drag me to a movie theater or restaurant. Strangely enough, there were times when I had no qualms about going places alone. Usually they were places where I felt some kind of solace—the library, the home-improvement store, the craft store, a museum—or could blend into the masses and be alone in a crowd, such as a different city or state.

In the aftermath of all the disappointments, hurdles, and handicaps of recent years, I have learned a lot about myself, and I have gained empathy and sympathy for others who have endured the medical trauma of a family member, being a caregiver, or suffering from mental, financial, or emotional distress. There is no worse feeling than being alone during a devastating event. No one should feel that.

I am still in the process of healing my own wounds, especially since my mother and I parted ways in April 2012. I won't go into details, as they are private. But suffice it to say, I am relieved from her toxic presence and never ending drama. Though a healthy decision with regards to self-preservation, afterward I needed to pursue healing. In the time since passed, I have read extensively and learned much about defining my childhood feelings, fears, and anxiety. Facing those has led me to grow mentally and emotionally.

I want to help others heal their wounds or improve their circumstances. In 2012, I volunteered for the Make-A-Wish Foundation, registered as a lifetime member of the National Kidney Foundation, and participated in a charity Walk to End Alzheimer's. I regularly donate blood at Red Cross functions. I am a registered organ donor through the Secretary of State for Michigan. I donate goods to local centers and those to be sent overseas to US soldiers. I feel my personal worth in doing acts of kindness for others without expectation of a return.

The events of our lives and the people involved in those events shape us. Although I can truly say I detest some of what I have had to endure to get to where I am today (spiritually, mentally, and physically), without a doubt I consider my soul richer and my mind wiser for having gone through the valleys. I still battle the ups and downs of depression, but by volunteering at a local library, keeping in touch with friends, and working in my yard, these things help boost my mood and sense of self-worth. My work in this world is not complete; I must "keep on keepin' on". And so do you.

Chapter 7

The Joy of Giving

People still ask me what I consider to be a silly question: "Does it feel weird . . . like, can you tell there's a part missing?"

My reply is always the same: "Um, *no.*"

My good friend Eugene, whom I've known for twenty years, had been on dialysis for several months in 2011 and was waiting to be placed on the kidney transplant list. I believe his renal function was at 9 percent, and three days each week were spent in a dialysis lab. It was slowly draining the life out of him. So when he texted me in August 2011 to say he finally made the list, I immediately asked him who I needed to contact to get an appointment to test my blood for a possible match in order to donate a kidney to him. I didn't have one second of hesitation.

The contact person in the transplant department at the hospital, Jack*, was absolutely great and easy to work with—a very professional, caring, and funny nurse coordinator. In the months to come, we would banter and chat on the phone, as well as when I came into the clinic for tests (and there were *many*). The whole team was great, actually, from the social workers to the surgeons.

After initial blood and urine tests to make sure I was disease-free and had good numbers for the urine components, I was called back for another blood test. This time, they were going to cross-match it with Eugene's and also test for tissue compatibility. Leaving that appointment, I had to complete a twenty-four-hour urine collection. While I was having all these donor tests done, Eugene was going through his own set of tests as the potential recipient.

It's hard to keep all the dates, appointments, and tests straight—there were so many! Both Eugene and I, along with our spouses, had to attend an evening seminar that covered the pluses and minuses of transplantation. Previous donors and recipients spoke about their experiences, and one of the team's doctors presented a slideshow and did a Q&A. We were given information packets following the presentation. A celebration luncheon was held every other year for transplant patients, we were told.

The next step for me was to spend the better part of an entire day in the transplant office. I was required to meet with everyone on the team before a decision could be made as to whether I was a good candidate. Even though all of my test results were great, the team could override those and rule that I wasn't, based on these interviews. Jack was very organized and the day went fairly smoothly. I spoke independently with each of the following in a private room: my living-donor advocate, the transplant social worker, the surgeon, a doctor of kidney nephrology, Jack, and a financial representative. In a way, I felt like I had to sell them on why I wanted to do this. I didn't figure on my good intentions being questioned to the degree they were. The team met the Friday after my appointment and agreed I was suitable donor material.

Next up was a round of more detailed and serious tests: CT angiogram scan (takes 3-D picture of kidneys), an EKG of my heart, and *more* blood work (it's a good thing I am not afraid of needles, plus I have *huge* veins and the "vampire" nurse was friendly). All of this was paid for by Eugene's insurance and/or covered by the hospital. Closer to surgery, I met with the urology resident and had one final meeting with Jack for a specific rundown on pre- and post surgery guidelines (drink water, no aspirin products, stop taking birth control, etc.).

I should state, I had never had an operation before in my life nor spent a night in the hospital for any illness of my own. I have visited many sick family and friends and been there for baby births. I practically lived at a different local hospital for six weeks three years earlier when Matt had his medical crisis. Considering that alone, one would think I would not be comfortable in a medical setting, especially as many visits as I made over the course of my four months of testing. However, I think that my comfort about my choice to donate, my limited knowledge of nursing, and the capability of the transplant team allowed me a feeling of excited ease.

Surgery day finally arrived: Wednesday, January 25, 2012. I got up when night was still cloaked in darkness in order to be at the hospital at five forty-five. I was too tired to feel hungry, thirsty, or nervous. Riding in the passenger seat as my husband drove, I was calm and quiet, but also in awe that, if all went well, I was going to be *saving Eugene's life* by the end of the day. Matt and I arrived at the hospital for surgical admission at the same time as Eugene and his family. Eugene and I were taken separately for operation preparation. Several of our family and friends worked at this hospital, and it was comforting that one cousin organized the pre-op duties and another cousin, her mother, came to check on me and stayed until I was taken into the operating room. Lying on the gurney in my pre-op room waiting for eight o'clock to arrive, I asked for a warm blanket and drifted in and out of sleep. No, I did not want to watch TV or have people back to visit; I was too sleepy. I'm dead on my feet without coffee. I longed for the bright overhead fluorescent lights to be turned off.

As the surgery time approached, one of my pastors and his associate came back to my prep room along with my mother, Matt, Anna, and my best girlfriend, Rachel. They actually made me nervous, sitting and standing around the room. They looked worried and teary-eyed as they stared at me. I was so mellow; I didn't want all that apprehensive energy around me. My dad ended up arriving just after the team hauled me away, so I didn't get to see him pre-op, which was kind of disappointing.

I remember the anesthesiologist coming into my prep room after everyone left, and she gave me some "happy juice" via my IV. After several minutes, I oddly felt no effect from the medicine. The OR team came for me, and I recall being wheeled through several bright, cold, white hallways and into an *enormous* operating room. It too was very bright; I recall white tiles and huge lamps. It kind of looked like I was time-traveling back to the 1960s.

A few nurses transferred me to a different bed. I was injected with another push of anesthesia, the oxygen mask went over my mouth and nose, and I drifted off fast. I think I made it as far as ninety-eight in my backward counting. Gone. I had been looking forward to this drug-induced nap all morning.

I woke up in a half-dark, semiprivate recovery area. I immediately recall hearing an irritating older man near me who was very chatty with the recovery nurse; I wished I had the strength to tell him to shut up. She was tending to both of us, urging me to wake up. Shortly, she brought my dad and Matt back to see me. I was so happy that Dad had made it. I remember feeling quite loopy and making crude but amusing hand gestures about Mr. Chatty to them. I was groggy, tired, and thirsty. Ice chips, please!

I was elated when the nurse said my private room was ready and I would be transported up to it soon. Good—no more Mr. Chatty. After the trip up to my room on the fifth floor, I got settled in, and a few family members stopped by my room that afternoon and evening to check on me. It really didn't matter to me who was there, I was so tired. But it felt good to be loved.

My first night, Wednesday, was not great. I had a migraine, so I had to ring for my nurse and wait for those meds. Every two hours at least, the nurse assistant came in to take my vitals. My nurse popped in to check on me and chart. I pushed the button on the Dilaudid pump whenever

I remembered. With too many people, lights, and stuff going on, I got a few hours of sleep at best.

The next morning, a family friend who works at the hospital came to see me and noticed urine on the floor to the right of my bed. She went to the nurse's station and asked for cleanup immediately. The nurse assistant of Night One had apparently missed the urine collector when emptying my urine bag and left a puddle for someone to step or slip in. That pissed me off (pun intended), and I was in such discomfort, sleep-deprived, and grumpy that everybody heard about it. I was supposed to get up and walk around Thursday to get rid of the surgery gases that had traveled to my shoulders, which hurt more than anything. What if I had stepped in that? What if I fell? Also, it meant she did not have a correct collection number for the volume of liquid I had output. It was not a great start to Thursday.

I had some more visitors as the day progressed, some people from church and the friends and family who worked at the hospital. I met the nutritionist who would make sure I received meals I actually liked and found appealing. Most importantly, I walked to the room of my kidney's recipient. Eugene was eating lunch. His room was smaller than mine, for which I felt bad. Mine was *huge*. Still, the sight of him brought me such joy! My catheter was taken out that morning by my daytime nurse assistant. Other than that, all I remember of Thursday is the incessant, almost debilitating gas pain in my shoulders and the feeling of weakness in my abdominal area where the doctor had cut through muscle.

Thursday night must have gone better, because I don't remember a whole lot. Maybe they just let me sleep. I know for sure I didn't have the same nurse assistant as the prior evening, because that was a demand made Thursday morning. I saw her walking in the hallway past my room during her shift, though, and I wanted to hurl something at her, only I didn't have the strength to.

Friday, my shoulders were a little better, but no matter, I had to do some *serious* walking that day. I took a shower, so thankful for the seat in the big, open bathroom! I felt much more alive afterward. I was having trouble with the breathing exercises that would help dissipate the gases. Jack and my donor advocate came by to see me; they knew Thursday would be bad for me, so they waited until Friday before paying a visit. Jack leaned over the bed railing and gave me a hug.

Several more friends and family members came by. Despite our age difference, Eugene and I oddly enough had a number of friends in common. Eugene walked to *my* room that afternoon while several people were visiting. Attached to his IV pole, he approached my bed with a mask over his nose and mouth and gently leaned over to give me a hug. People were snapping photos and getting emotional. I was so happy to see him walking around! He felt better, and I'd had a hand in that.

Eugene stayed and visited for a short while before retiring to his room because of fatigue. Rachel came to see me that afternoon and kept me company while Matt and my mom got dinner outside of the hospital setting. Toward the end of visiting hours, people we knew who were more Eugene's friends than mine came by to see me. They all pretty much wanted to say the same thing: "Thank you." Middle-aged men got quite emotional about this event. I still don't get why people made such a big deal of this. I didn't feel like much had been done to me (other than pumping me excessively full of gas). It was my pleasure and honor to donate my kidney. The only thank-you I needed was to see Eugene have a dialysis-free life, with more energy, and have his hilarious personality return.

I don't remember Friday night, but I believe I got around six hours of sleep, which I was thrilled about. Saturday morning, I was eating breakfast when Matt arrived. We soon got me out of bed to shower, and then the nurse assistant came by to check my vitals. An associate of the surgeon checked on me and made the determination that I could go home Saturday. My nurse began the discharge paperwork. I didn't even get to eat the lunch I ordered before everything was in order for my release. I don't remember what I had ordered, but it sounded good, and I was *really* disappointed I didn't get to eat it!

As Matt and I were getting my belongings together, Eugene and his wife, Gerri, came by my room with a photographer friend of theirs. Eugene was going home too—I couldn't believe he was being discharged so soon! Everyone on the transplant team had said he could be in the hospital up to a week. I was amazed he could leave earlier than that. But my kidney was working really well in him, so our doctor felt comfortable discharging him.

Since Eugene is Chinese, I had Matt purchase a small bamboo plant in a pot in reciprocation for the beautiful bouquet of roses and lilies he sent to me on Thursday. Gerri hugged me, crying, and all she could say was thank you. I know they were tears of joy and gratitude, but I felt bad that she was crying. I leaned over to hug Eugene, and he was overcome as well. My wheelchair transport then arrived, and we were both escorted downstairs, where we waited in the lobby together while our spouses retrieved our cars via the valet.

I was glad to go home but apprehensive of how good of a caretaker Matt would be. Well, I needn't have worried: he was quite good, for a man. He got me food, helped me shower and walk around, gave me meds, and kept the house up. Some friends came a few evenings to bring dinners for us and to see how I was doing. I received many cards and a few plants and flowers. Jack called to follow-up on how I was feeling. It was hard sleeping in a regular bed the first few nights. I wasn't used to being flat with my freshly cut abdominal muscles pulled straight. I longed to sleep on my side, but I knew I had a few days before my body would be ready to tolerate that. So I propped myself up with a few pillows instead.

By the end of the first week home, I was feeling significantly better. The transplant doctor had to see me in his office that week for post-op follow-up. He was pleased with my mobility and the look and feel of my scar. (By the way, even though he sutured from the inside, on the outside he put this purple/bluish skin glue that itched something awful! I couldn't wait for it to all slough off. Plus I was anxious to see my actual scar underneath.) I was submitted to a final blood and urine test that day; when my copies of the results arrived, they showed normal ranges. I was sad I wouldn't be a regular at the transplant office anymore. I was going to miss the people—they were all so nice. But the built-up excitement was over, and it was time to move on and get better.

After two weeks, I was ready to be out in public. It was a rare mild Michigan winter and we had a large home at the time, but cabin fever had weaseled in on me. I attended church, and people were amazed to see me and that I looked so good—like nothing happened, I suppose they meant. I started to go on errands sporadically. For six weeks, I wasn't allowed to carry anything heavier than ten pounds, so I was able to avoid laundry and groceries, much to my pleasure.

A few months post-op, when both Eugene and I were feeling rather normal, Matt and I met him and Gerri for lunch: dim sum, our favorite double-date food. Eugene had lost about thirty pounds, and his funny, chatty personality had returned. His wife was so pleased to see him this way. I think that meal was one of the best of my life.

I registered as a living kidney donor with the National Kidney Foundation (NKF) shortly after the operation. Because I am a donor, if my other kidney blows out, I get placed at the top of the national transplant list. (Kind of cool to be a VIP.) I also registered with the State of Michigan to be an organ and tissue donor.

I formed a small team for a NKF walk in June 2012 and collected five hundred dollars from friends and family. Eugene, Gerri, and their son and daughter walked with Matt and me in Lansing. Our team was named Mushu on the Move. Here's the story behind that: Eugene is Chinese, his name in Chinese means dragon, and the year of the dragon started around the time of the operation. Mushu is the small dragon in the Disney animated feature *Mulan*, one of my favorite Disney movies. So when we decided to come up with a name for our mutual kidney, Mushu seemed like an obvious choice. When I inquire as to how Eugene's doing, I ask, "How's Mushu working for ya?" Or he'll inform me, "Mushu woke me up last night at two in the morning to pee." It's our inside joke. Eugene even had special orange T-shirts made by a friend for our walk group displaying a dragon and our team name.

Eugene's life has more than likely been extended from two years without a transplant to up to twenty years because of the donation, based on statistics. The fact he received a kidney from a living donor is also in his favor. He is a music teacher at a private Christian school and plays the saxophone statewide at weddings, parties, corporate events, and restaurants. He has gotten his wind back and is booking and playing gigs again. He returned to school to finish the 2011–2012 school year.

On October 13, 2012, Eugene, Gerri, Matt, and I attended the hospital's recognition party for transplant donors and recipients. When I was confirming my RSVP with the kidney-transplant office, I told the social worker that Eugene was back to playing his sax as good as ever. I mentioned this only because she said there would be a pianist at the event, and I thought it would be very inspiring for other attendees to see and hear Eugene play along.

And play he did—one song dedicated to me and one for the transplant team. There wasn't a dry eye in the room. I was very touched, and continue to be, by Eugene's undying gratefulness. Each donor and recipient received a small "goodie bag" thanks to a local artist in attendance. We had pictures taken with nurse Jack, our surgeon, and with some other members of the transplant office staff. Afterward, the four of us went out for a *real* meal (we're incurable "foodies") to celebrate in our own fashion. Actually, should we ever stop celebrating, or cherishing, this remarkable event? I don't think so.

For years, I'd talked about getting a tattoo. I couldn't decide what I wanted to have permanently inked on my body. And where would it go? I didn't want it somewhere really exposed. One winter evening, I met a girlfriend and her kids for dinner and decided, for whatever reason, that this was the night. My friend had several tattoos, so she would be the perfect hand-holder for this novice.

I chose the Chinese language symbol for "give" and had the artist mark me on my lower left abdomen, just south of my kidney surgery scar. Because some of the nerves in that area were numb, it tickled when the ink pen vibrated against my skin. I tried not to giggle. When he reached my hipbone, it actually hurt a little, but it was tolerable and over quickly. My girlfriend kindly took photos of my various facial expressions during the process. In less than thirty minutes, I had my first tattoo, which means more to me than any other design I had previously thought of.

On the cold Michigan afternoon of January 16, 2013, Eugene and I met each other at the school where he teaches music theory and band. Together we rode to the administration building of the hospital where we'd had our operations and were greeted by an employee who led us to the auditorium. A fifth-grade class was waiting inside along with some mothers, transplant-department staff members, and camera operators. Eugene and I were going to be interviewed by the kids; they were entering their video in some kind of contest, and to prepare, they had been studying about organ transplants for weeks.

While we waited for our turn, the students interviewed one of the social workers with the transplant team. I secretly hoped the brisk wind hadn't ruined my good hair day. Eugene and I chatted with hospital staff members we knew, and before we knew it, it was our turn to be in the hot seat. The two of us sat next to each other on highly elevated office chairs on a white stage with a satiny white fabric draped as a backdrop. With the bright lights on us, it was like walking into an opaline clamshell. A cameraman clipped microphones on us like the news anchors wear. The Q&A went by quickly. I wasn't sure whether to look at the camera or the student asking the questions, so I did both. Since Eugene was a teacher, he seemed more comfortable than I was in front of a small crowd.

Afterward, the mothers were very good about making sure all of the students came up to us to say thank you and shake our hands. Some of the moms were even teary-eyed, which was humbling. They couldn't believe how generous it was for me to donate my kidney. I felt awkward and just kind of shrugged the importance and attention off, eschewing the seriousness of the moment. As they gathered around him, Eugene showed the children some post-op pictures of us, which they seemed interested in. We were each given a thank-you card from the students, which included a picture of them and all their signatures. Eugene asked one of the hospital staff members if we could receive a copy of the interview in its entirety, and she said yes.

As stated at the beginning of this story, I had no second thoughts or hesitation about doing this act. The Bible says to love your neighbor as yourself and that one who lays down his life for another is the greatest example of God's love. I wasn't thinking about these verses when I called Jack for the first time. My reaction was purely instinctual: *My friend needs help—I wonder if I can help him.* I didn't think that my life was in danger for undergoing this procedure. Others started to quote those scriptures and wanted to put me on another level, it seemed. I'm just a person who had an organ to spare and was lucky enough to be a healthy match. I played the donation down because I figured anyone would do that for a friend. But I would learn that not everyone would, can, or does.

The magnitude of my opportunity to influence and improve Eugene's life weighed on me close to the surgery date. I felt so honored that, since I was the first and only person tested for compatibility, it seemed God specifically chose me for this opportunity. Why me? Who indeed but someone who humbly and purely wanted to help her friend? I did this great thing not for acknowledgement or attention, but because I didn't need my left kidney—the right one works perfectly fine. For me, it was like sharing your school lunch with a friend: "Oh, your mom packed you *that*? Here, have some of mine instead." Eugene's story would be different, but through my eyes and heart, all I did was share my sandwich with him.

Chapter 8

Coach Courageous

My dad is a modern-day Renaissance man. He taught middle-school history, coached several sports, and has been mayor of a small Michigan town. He has experience with plumbing, painting, electrical, and woodworking, and he can do amazing (and stupid) things with duct tape. As an athletic man, he has participated in bowling, baseball, wrestling, roller-skating, volleyball, and pickleball, and he also knows personal defense. He's had odd summer jobs as a house painter, coached several after-school sports (both boys' and girls' teams), and was a community activities director out of college. During Vietnam, he was stationed in West Germany while in the Army with top-secret clearance. He has visited most of western Europe and half of the United States. He even knows how to use his mom's outdated sewing machine!

With a list of accomplishments and qualities like that, I wondered how he would cope with retirement after thirty-two years of teaching. I thought he might be one of those people who wouldn't know what do with themselves or the extra free time. I accompanied him to the retirement dinner party held for several school-district employees. A slide show included pictures of the staff through the years, and seeing my dad with shaggy brown hair (not a grey buzz cut) in a beige sport coat and fit as a fiddle was a memory flashback! It sure transported me back to 1980.

Despite my concerns, he seemed to ease into retirement gracefully: substitute teaching once in a while for extra cash, playing golf twice a week, occasionally working the small precinct elections, joining the local senior center to play volleyball, and walking his two dogs daily. As active as he was, I had a nagging fear his health wasn't on par. He had become a bit overweight in recent years and was on blood-pressure medicine. I figured it was residual from his quitting smoking and years of stress.

He was less than forthcoming about any information regarding his aging body. (Are all older parents like that?) When he told me he passed a funky-looking three-inch "something" through his urethra the summer of 2012, I became more alert and concerned. I pressured him to get it lab-tested and to keep all his doctor appointments (he had a lovely habit of cancelling them because "I feel fine"). The hypervigilance from Matt's medical scare resurfaced, and Advocate Stacy kicked in.

The unknown thing he passed was actually a blood clot! Dad's urologist scheduled outpatient surgery at the local hospital about two months later. I did not know the name or purpose of the procedure; Dad just told me he needed someone to drive him home and spend the night. The morning of the procedure, we drove quietly to the nearby hospital. I checked him in at the volunteer desk in the surgical waiting room. Shortly thereafter, a nurse called his name and took him back to the pre-op area. I had brought a book with me but didn't feel like reading; I was edgy. After a surprise short visit with Dad before the anesthesiologist put him under, I went to the food court to get coffee and breakfast, and then I camped out in the modern orange waiting room for the remainder of the morning, tuning out the voices of the fellow patients' families waiting nearby and the perky morning news reporters on the televisions.

The urologist called me into a private consultation room after he finished Dad's operation. The first thing he asked me was if Dad smoked. I told him no, not for a decade, but prior to that, yes. He nodded and pulled out his phone with a picture on it. Displayed was a roundish mass, pink and turquoise in color, with crystalline tips. My mind immediately jumped to images from science class or CSI television shows. Thrusting this foreign image toward me, the doctor said "Cancer." My stomach dropped.

He went on to inform me that he had removed the entire mass and scraped at the bottom of the bladder wall (where the mass had attached itself) to ensure no cells were left behind, but if the cells were deep into the muscle wall, there was nothing he could do for treatment. He would know more after the pathology report came out in about two weeks. At my request, the doctor drew a somewhat detailed picture of what the bladder looks like and the surgery he had performed. I am a visual person, so this helped me understand.

Shortly after that, the doctor left the room and shut the door, and I proceeded to break down in tears. Thoughts and feelings came fast and in no certain order. *Not Dad! I haven't spent enough time with him! He's too young! This isn't fair—I don't want any more medical traumas to help someone through. I'm not strong enough for this. He's my only parent. What about my younger half- sister? She's too young to not have Dad around.* I sobbed as I called Matt to tell him the news. He said he would call my sister and ask her to drive over and be with me. And then, surprisingly, he drove to the hospital, too.

The doctor didn't tell Dad in recovery that day that a cancerous tumor had been removed from his bladder. My sister and I sure didn't want to be the bearer of such news, not knowing what the pathology report would reveal. So we kept our mouths shut. Dad's nurse in the post-op area was surprised at how the doctor was (not) handling the situation, and I kindly made it known to her that I was not happy with his behavior. She didn't blame me and gave me a sympathetic look.

Of course, I spent the next few weeks reflecting on memories of Dad and me. He had been a "weekend father," so our moments together were limited—between the parental agreement from his divorce from my mother and my desire to avoid my crazy stepmom. He and I escaped from the house for fun activities when possible; neither of us liked to be still unless we were reading or very ill. Fun memories of "just us" included roller skating at a local rink and playing "crack the whip" to 80s music with his students who happened to be there; viewing movies (I cried at *The Last Unicorn*); going bowling for a few games; washing and waxing his car in the summer; and bike-riding through the small town he lived in. While we awaited the results of the pathology report, I dug into those childhood memories and held them tight, torturing myself should the news be bad.

I met Dad at the urologist's office for the results a few weeks later. It was indeed a cancerous tumor, but there were no cells in the bladder muscle wall. It was Stage 1 bladder cancer. Just as a precaution, the doctor ordered Dad to six weeks of BCG (Bacillus Calmette-Guérin) treatments, to be followed by a cystogram six weeks after the final treatment.

In the weeks that followed, I made a routine of driving over to Dad's house on Thursday and staying through Saturday. His treatments were on Friday afternoons, and he was to go home and lie down for two hours. He also needed to be watched for any side effects that might develop, some of which could be severe. I was his chauffeur and his home aide. Dad would make off-color jokes to me about the nurses dealing with his man bits, and while some daughters might be grossed out, I just rolled my eyes and chuckled. What a goof. That corny humor must have been one way he was dealing with the weekly appointments. He didn't say much about it otherwise. Dad ended up not experiencing any side effects (I have no doubt due in part to my church family and friends praying for him) unless he hid them from me.

I came to enjoy my regular visits to his ranch home in the small old town he used to run. The house that I used to not feel welcome in when he was with my former stepmom (before she up and left him without notice) was becoming more of a second home to me. I added some updated pictures to the guest bedroom where I slept, and performed a cheap facelift of the main bathroom with some grey paint and matching accessories. I think he got used to me being around more and liked it, despite my quirkiness he never realized existed until then.

I purged his fridge and cupboards of expired foods. I rearranged some kitchen drawers for more feng-shui convenience. Even his small dogs got used to me; they would lavish me with attention when I arrived on Thursday and pout when I left on Saturday. One of the dogs would sit outside my bedroom door and whine for me until I woke up in the mornings. Once up, my morning ritual with Dad was to sit across from him at the dining table, our laptops back to back, while we read the news, ate a small breakfast, e-mailed, chatted, and checked out videos of our favorite musicians on YouTube.

On a cold Midwestern February morning, Dad and I drove to the urologist's office. This was it: D-day. The cystogram would determine if his BCG treatments were effective and whether all the cancer cells (if any remained after surgery) were gone. I wanted to be in the room with Dad when his doctor examined him and told him the results. If it was bad news, I did not want him to be alone; no one should be alone for something like that. But he said he wanted to go in by himself. I had to respect his decision.

During the half hour Dad was back with the doctor, to say I was anxious and nervous is an understatement. My mind was a scrambled mess of thoughts and emotions, and I couldn't concentrate on my iPhone games or the waiting-room magazines. I eavesdropped on the clerical staff's banter for distraction. Sitting with my legs crossed, twitching and swinging the top leg, I was full of several months' worth of adrenaline. Then Dad opened the door from the back. He wore a poker face, with me looking at him expectantly. He leaned over to grab his coat from the chair next to me, bent down to my ear, and whispered, "I'm all clear."

Thank you Jesus! I wanted to scream and jump up and down right there in the waiting room. We put our coats on, playing it cool, but the minute we left the building, I gave him the biggest, tightest, most grateful hug. He gave me a good bear hug back. My sister and I would have our dad around longer than we had recently thought. Dad's not one to celebrate much and underplays many situations, but I asked him if there was anything he'd like to do the rest of the day to celebrate. He simply wanted to go to the local mall and walk around with me and have lunch.

Dad isn't big on any "higher power" concept, but he did comment that all the prayers must have helped. I knew it was so. He may have put up a brave front, as I suppose any aging parent would. But knowing him as I do, I know that in his own way, he was worried. I picked up on little hints in things he said and odd reading materials lying around the house (like pamphlets about probate estates). The biggest realization I had was that my dad—this man who had accomplished so much with his life and made a difference to so many people, who was someone I looked up to and as a child thought was Superman—was, at the end of the day, just a man, vulnerable to medical issues like any of us. Facing his possible mortality sobered up my sister, Dad, and me a bit.

Dad has been a "tough guy" all his life, but when the rubber met the road with this cancer scare, I believe his perspective changed a bit. Cancer can do that. He began to slowly change his diet and went almost cold turkey on withdrawing from soda pop. His sodium, cholesterol, and blood pressure numbers came down as a result. He didn't have to act strong for me or my sister; it's just in his nature to be a tough guy. His courageous cover was blown, though, and it was more than okay that the former Army sergeant/teacher/coach/mayor showed his underbelly a little.

Along with organ donation and patient rights, I now also support cancer causes. To those of you who have not been as fortunate in your (or a family member's) cancer journey, and I know there are millions, believe me when I say that I empathize and feel a burden for you. I have watched this disease destroy the bodies of my relatives, church members, and my best friend's mother.

At Dad's one-year checkup recently, the urologist determined that his bladder looked healthy. Next up is a kidney test in the spring. In collusion with the past year's concerns, the relationship I have with my dad has never been healthier. We share information, emotions - a lot of things that we were once too proud to say. He is one of my best friends. I am more like him than I ever thought. The wall has come down. Courage sometimes takes on the form of vulnerability, not just being "tough".

Travel

CHAPTER 9

Dare to Do

I began making and pursuing my bucket list at age thirty. Not necessarily because I had reason to believe my days were numbered or had started feeling a deep sense of my own mortality, but because it seemed like I was having a minor prelude to a midlife crisis or something. I felt like I had accomplished so little in my time on earth thus far. I had a "seize the day" mentality, determined to try new things, take risks, and fulfill some dreams. Some of my adventures were of the cheaper sort; some were a bit pricier.

I had lived in the greater Detroit area since 1993, but I was often afraid or unwilling to give myself over to the location. It was time to delve into the local culture. That included trying ethnic foods, attending local sporting events, expanding my appreciation for the arts, and driving in a strange and crime-rich city. For a few years, I was a member at the Detroit Institute of Arts and the Detroit Zoo; I was also a frequent visitor to MOCAD (Museum of Contemporary Art Detroit) and the Detroit Film Institute. I attended lectures at area libraries. Two girlfriends and I attended the opera *Turandot.* At theaters nearby, *Stomp* blew my mind, and at *Avenue Q,* I nearly peed myself due to extensive laughter. I attended several baseball games at

Comerica Park. I'd always been a baseball fan and discovered I loved watching it live as opposed to on television, despite loud drunken fans and misbehaved children. For a few summers, I was a "voucher junkie" for concerts at DTE Energy Music Theater and Meadowbrook (both outdoor venues). My love for muscle cars was renewed when I attended the annual Woodward Dream Cruise and Detroit International Auto Show, as well as visiting the Walter P. Chrysler Museum.

My husband, Matt, scheduled a hot-air balloon ride for my thirtieth birthday present. It was an early-morning ride a few days after my actual birthday, in the first week of July, and the quietness of the air as we floated through space was magical. Our direction and speed were at the mercy of thermal air pockets and breeze. It was so different seeing familiar towns and iconic buildings from that vantage point. The countryside was a patchwork of subdivisions, farmland, golf courses, and concrete. We coasted in the air for a glorious hour or more before our bumpy landing in a field.

In the span of a few years, I went parasailing twice—once in Florida at Disney World and the other in the Straits of Mackinac. The Disney adventure with Matt was more enjoyable: we had better weather, we could see downtown Orlando from Bay Lake at the Contemporary Hotel, and the cord let us fly higher than when I flew in the cloudy Straits with our cousin. The only sound was the cord vibrating with tension as the small boat pulled us; otherwise, it was blessed peace, a light wind in my face, and a spectacular view.

Also while in Florida one winter, Matt and I snorkeled with manatees. We made a reservation with Bird's Underwater in Crystal River, and had to be there very early the morning of our excursion – 6:30, I believe. There was a group of about 10 people going out on the pontoon manned by a female captain, who was an expert diver. We watched a video on manatee safety and the regulations of swimming with them, as they are a protected species. Finding an appropriate-fitting full body neoprene dive suit was interesting. After all were armed with information and snorkels and flippers, the boat set off down the quiet river on what was to be a lovely sunny day.

After the captain found a good location (using her years of skills and experience), we all geared up and slipped into the cool water. It took me probably 15 minutes to practice breathing through the snorkel mouth tube, as it was instinct to want to use my nose instead. But no, one has to only use the mouth and fill those lungs with precious air in order to stay and swim beneath the surface. Kicking using flippers was an awkward experience as well. Snorkeling was like 'riding a bike' for Matt, as several years prior he had earned his diver's certification, and I was glad for tips he gave me. I warmed up as the insulation provided by the dive suit warmed the river water trapped between it and my skin.

A few manatees gathered near our group. Per the instructions, we could only use one hand at a time to touch them. They were so docile; they rolled over and over in the water, turning for a specific body area to be rubbed. Obviously they were accustomed to people. A few had scars, and most has clumps of algae on their bodies. Their grey-ish brown skin was rubbery to touch, soft with a toughness or thickness to it. The sweet mammals' dark eyes melted my heart. Some manatees would even reach out a front flipper, as if to shake your hand or give a high-five. It was clear they loved the attention.

In an unexpected yet amazing 'detour' of sorts, several of us in the group swam through a craggy-treed stream which led to a deep, open pool where many fish congregated. It was a struggle to navigate the stream in gear I wasn't used to, but "the hole", as it was called, was amazing. The water was as blue as the Caribbean Sea, and there was indeed a depression in the earth that seemed out of place in the otherwise fairly shallow waters. We swam in this cove for awhile, Matt and I motioning to each other and trying to communicate underwater about the beautiful scenery and fish.

While the group was snorkeling for three hours, our captain was also in the water, using a special underwater dive camera to record footage of the manatees and our precious time with them. She also provided additional information and aided us adventurers so our experience was a memorable one. During the ride back to the launch, most of us peeled out of our dive suits to dry off and soak up some Florida sun. The adrenaline rush I had been on since early morning was wearing off quickly. After purchasing a copy of the captain's video footage from our snorkel experience, Matt and I ate lunch at a nearby restaurant, and looked out upon the manatee-filled river.

Also in this awakening of sorts, I decided to travel a bit. Nothing major at first. One long weekend in November, a girlfriend and I flew to New York City. Our hotel was a block from Broadway in Midtown, so at night we heard car horns and fire-truck sirens, although the real noisemaker was the defunct window-unit air-conditioner. The city was freaking cold, it rained half the time, and we didn't get to see all the sights we wanted (how can you, in three days?), nor did we get in to Serendipity for their famous frozen hot chocolate. It was a great experience nonetheless. I loved just walking the streets or riding the subway, blending in with the city, feeling its rhythm and pulse. Seeing Ground Zero while it was still fenced off and being cleaned up was something I will never forget, and visiting the United Nations was pretty incredible. The Vietnamese restaurant that my professor friend John recommended we eat lunch at in Chinatown was quite yummy. He had lived in New York City for roughly two decades, so I sought his counsel beforehand.

Another long weekend was spent with some girlfriends in Chicago one July. My grandmother had just passed away a few weeks earlier, and I knew she and my grandfather had honeymooned in the Windy

City, so I was determined to locate the Palmer House Hotel where they stayed. It turned out to be right in front of me one day as we were walking to lunch in the Loop. I didn't, or couldn't, go inside, but just knowing she and I had stood in the same section of town decades apart made her feel close by once again.

We bought three-day bus/metro passes and made good use of them for our short trip. Our destinations included the Hancock Tower, Shedd Aquarium, Chicago Art Institute, Museum of Natural History, Millennium Park, and the Museum of Science and Industry. We ate at the Corner Bakery, Ed Debevic's, the Cheesecake Factory, and Pizzeria Uno. Navy Pier at night was an awesome experience, but unfortunately we were not able to get on the Ferris wheel for a ride. (A good reason for a return visit, no?) We boldly ventured to the South Side to eat dinner in Chinatown. A guided boat tour up the river and out into the harbor was a great way to gain some local history and get a great view of Chicago and its landmarks. Our hotel had a rooftop deck, so late each evening, we would sneak up there in the dark and listen to the city sounds, enjoy the twinkle of building lights against the black sky, feel the warm breeze caress our skin after a hot day, and act as voyeurs peeking into the open windows of nearby apartments.

Somehow, one summer I talked Matt into a short-notice trip to West Virginia for white-water rafting. We had just returned from our annual camping summer vacation, and I was left unfulfilled. I did some Internet research and made reservations at Ace Adventure Center for September. The nine-hour drive proved slow-paced as we made our way through Ohio, but tree-decked hills, winding highways, and small blue-collar towns revealed themselves as we journeyed southeast toward our destination.

The morning of our river ride was foggy and a bit chilly, and I was very nervous. We suited up in neoprene dive suits and plastic helmets, grabbed our life vests and paddles, then boarded the bus for the put-in site. The river was calm, with mostly Class I and Class II rapids. It was a beautiful day, and watching the morning fog gently lift from the green hills surrounding us was like observing an ethereal veil lift from nature's stage.

I had imagined we would be in a raft with at least six to eight people, but in reality, ours was much smaller (and easier to fall out of, I thought). The only other passengers were a couple from North Carolina and Randy, our guide. Randy was the epitome of a mountain man: thin and muscular, with a scraggly beard. This middle-aged man worked the rivers in the summer and the ski resorts in the off-season. He knew all about the local history, explaining and pointing out things as we paddled along. "See that train track there? Well . . ." or "That rock formation was actually . . ."

We took our raft ashore for lunch. Another raft that was alongside us for the trip joined us, and the guides unpacked a feast of sandwiches, salads, and desserts. We were all ravenously hungry. The outhouse at the picnic site was scarier than the mild rapids I had encountered already; all I could think was, "This is *not* where I want to get bitten by a mystery spider and slowly die a poisonous death." Ever tried peeling out of a wet wetsuit? I should have just wandered into the shallow riverbed nearby (which went under an old railroad trestle), squatted, and pissed myself in the suit.

The afternoon portion of the trip was mostly Class II and III rapids, with a few Class IVs thrown in for good measure. The man with us from North Carolina popped out of the raft when we caught a hole in one rapids, and Randy did some quick maneuvering so we could all help him back in. The man was chuckling about it, but the danger of what we were doing crept back into my imagination.

Mid afternoon, we reached a huge rock on the side of the river, and the current wasn't too strong, so we paused for a few minutes along with our companion raft. Randy said people could jump off the rock if they wanted to; the river was high enough that it was safe. A young couple from the other raft disembarked and scrambled behind and up to the top of the round, three-story mineral mass. On a split-second whim (or a burst of momentary insanity), I decided to follow suit. Matt was shocked, and even Randy seemed surprised, but I removed my shoes and helmet and climbed the rock.

The guides kept the rafts circling while the few daredevils took the leap of faith. I was last to jump. I perched my feet on the edge of the round rock top, took a quick look down to what would either be my death or liberation, took a deep breath, plugged my nose, and stepped off the edge. The feeling of the free fall was awesome, short, and scary. I hit the water at a slight angle, so my right butt cheek and thigh took a hard smack as I broke through the surface and plunged a questionable amount of feet into the river's depths. Between the cool water temperature and the pain of my leg and butt, I was nearly rendered breathless—not a good thing while trying to swim up to the surface. I received applause from the whole group when my head popped out of the river, and assistance from my raftmates in climbing back on board.

The last portion of the trip went by really fast as we paddled the higher level rapids. Randy shouted instructions ahead of time, warned us about "holes," and yelled for us to "paddle, paddle, paddle" right or left while in the midst of a rapid. The very last rapid/hole/trick-of-death was a scattered formation of boulders in the middle of the river named "Thread the Needle." Why Randy told us that *before* we attacked it, I'll never know. It was a definite Class IV. The anticipation was, again, worse than actually going through it. We paddled under direction, got soaked, and laughed when it was over. Adrenaline rush!

After that final battle against Mother Nature, the river was calm and smooth, and we slowly approached the New River Gorge Bridge, a sight to behold from our vantage point. The sun and water now felt warm under the drying neoprene suit, and I couldn't wait to take off my helmet. I used my plastic waterproof camera to take various pictures. As we approached the take-out area for the rafts, the bus was waiting for us. Tour employees loaded it up and drove the bumpy road through the West Virginia woods back to camp. Cold pops and beers were passed around as we all shared our individual tales of conquering the river, adrenaline still pumping through our bodies. We had all gotten a little braver that day, subjecting ourselves to the mercy and untamed wilderness of the New River.

Not only did some of these journeys fulfill something inside me, they awoke something as well: my desire to travel and experience new things. Not boring new things—extraordinary new things. Though not a roller-coaster freak, I do consider myself something of an adrenaline junkie. But like any junkie, I am always looking for my next experience, my next fix. Will I ever be satisfied, my thirst quenched? I would be seriously disappointed if it came to that.

Chapter 10

Twelve States, Eleven Days, Five Thousand Miles

I just decided to go. The notion of making a solo road trip had been simmering in my brain for a few weeks. For me, that's fairly impromptu. It was something I *needed*, in a deep, soulful, mind-broadening way. The wide-open road was whispering my name. I was up for the challenge.

Since I was not working, I would have to be really frugal with money, but time was not an issue. I decided to drive west and to parallel Route 66 as closely as I could, yet stick to major highways. Las Vegas was my destination. I wanted to see the Hoover Dam and hike Red Rock Canyon, things I didn't have the opportunity to do when I'd visited in 2009 (right before "the Event"). The route back to Michigan was undecided and open-ended. I had few real plans, so I had the freedom to make stops whenever and wherever I wanted.

Matt had progressed in his recovery as much as his body would allow. His endurance, strength, and appetite were much improved. He was approved for monthly Social Security benefits since his condition no longer allowed him to perform the laborious tasks of the only job he ever held. Days were usually spent around the house, though he regularly visited his mom and other family members. I felt no hesitation in leaving him.

My red Chevy Cruze was packed to the gills with clothes for any weather. I wanted to be prepared for anything, so I brought everything from hiking clothes to trendy Vegas outfits to a winter parka to a bathing suit just in case I came across a hotel with a pool. A twenty-four-pack of bottled water was in my trunk along with my suitcase. My toiletry bag and shoe bag were both on the floor of the backseat. The backseat itself was covered with a fleece blanket and a bed pillow in case I had to sleep in the car, along with four different coats and a stuffed Snoopy. The backseat would also become the periodicals rack for the trip. I tend to hoard maps and pamphlets; I'll blame that on my scrapbooking hobby.

On the front passenger floor was my market basket filled with non-perishable items, some fruit, energy bars, and the like. The passenger seat was Navigation Central: my GPS, Rand McNally US/state-by-state roadmap, iPhone, camera, purse, sunglasses, mace, pen, and ChapStick.

The Chevy and I left home around eight thirty in the morning on October 30, 2011. I was thirty six years old and had never done anything like this before. The speedometer read 5,708 miles. It was a clear and sunny morning, but cold at 35 degrees. I didn't have any weird travel butterflies like you might expect. Here was this huge, unknown, anything-can-happen journey before me, and I was . . . relaxed. Ready for the challenge and experiences this trip would bring. I kept a medium-sized spiral notebook in the navigation seat so I could quickly jot down observations as I came upon them. (There's not a law against taking notes while driving, is there? Oops, then.)

While still within Michigan borders, I passed three dead deer on I-94 West and drove past two cow-transport trucks on I-69 South/

West. Both made me sad. I encountered a moron in a Corvette twice my age with road rage like I'd never seen before—and it was apparently aimed at me! He was driving very erratically and really started to scare me, so I called 911 and reported him. I have no idea if he got stopped farther down the road, but I was not going to let him think that dangerous and stupid behavior would be tolerated. What a jackwagon.

Once in Indiana, the adventure really began. A party store named the Butt Hut caught my attention, even though I am a nonsmoker myself. I believe it was somewhere near Indianapolis. I spotted a town's water tower that read "Gas City." (Really, now?) As far as corporate America goes, I passed three headquarters while in the Hoosier state: the Nestle factory with a huge waving bunny near the freeway, Tractor Supply Co. (every man's dream), and Sallie Mae (one of the private lending investor companies).

Westbound I-70 was under construction and down to one lane. Let me state, I am not a fan of the orange barrels. In Michigan, they are out all year long, obstructing any road you may possibly want to drive down, as well as several alternate routes. So I tend to have a certain fast and hostile reaction to anything orange. But one redeeming sight I beheld in Indiana was an open Stuckey's, which of course I stopped at, getting the necessary nonessentials and going on my merry way, feeling nostalgic for my youth.

I started to feel like I was really gaining mileage once I reached eastern Illinois. Refilled the gas tank in Marshall at 3:20 p.m. Drove past a semitrailer that belonged to the Batesville Casket Company with the tag line: "Drive Safely—Heaven Can Wait." (Tell that to my road rage pal please!) I was catching on pretty quickly that I was going to encounter some quirky stuff in the coming days. Around Effingham, there was a huge metal Christian cross along the freeway. I mentally paused and reflected about the freedom that we, as a nation, have to display that. Saw two more dead deer. I'd rather have them shot by hunters and used for food than mangled and then ditched along the freeway; seems like such a waste of life to me. Stopped in Vandalia, Illinois, at a Lincoln historical site. There stood a large white courthouse with four wide round columns where Honest Abe argued a case early on in his legal career. The day was cloudy and a bit chilly, plus the courthouse was closed, so I pressed onward.

I reached St. Louis, Missouri, in evening rush hour, on top of which there was some big sporting event downtown, so people and cars were *everywhere.* I slowly crept my way to the Gateway Arch, but the National Park Service had already closed it up for the day. I was quite bummed; riding to the top of that monument was on my bucket list, and since I had no planned route, I wasn't sure if I'd be coming back through on my way home. I took several pictures of the architectural marvel and then, with grey skies looming overhead and the wind picking up, I decided it was time to forge ahead, disappointed though I was. I drove to Sullivan, Missouri, where I spent the night in a dreadful (but cheap) hotel. I shuddered at the thought of what a CSI's blue light might reveal. Ugh. I took a photo of the old Diamond Inn Motel lit in neon.

Halloween morning, I departed the motel at eight o'clock, with my odometer reading 6,370 miles. The terrain was starting to become a tad hilly, different from the usual flatness of the Midwest. I passed a recreational sign for Pomme de Terre Lake—those of us who remember some high-school French know that translates to Potato Lake. This raised many questions in my overly analytical brain, ones I didn't necessarily need answered by making a visit to said lake. Midmorning, I came upon a Case knife outlet store in a pole barn just off the freeway. I was beyond excited to discover this gem! The hubby's gun and knife obsession had taught me what to appreciate and what was crap. Case was not crap. Plus, it's an American company. Almost two hours later, after an excessive amount of texting, e-mailing of photos, and finally talking with Matt, he decided on the knife he wanted me to purchase for him. I was aggravated by how much road time that stop took from me. My blood sugar had dropped, and I was starving!

Whizzing by factories like Peterbilt and French's Mustard, I spotted a sign for Lambert's Cafe—"Home of the Throwed Rolls." It was a ten-minute detour to Ozark from my planned route for the day, but since I'd seen the restaurant on cable TV shows, there wasn't an option of not going. The building was as big as a Cracker Barrel from the outside. I was cheerfully seated at a booth and offered fried okra, and soon I placed my order—sweet tea, chicken-fried steak, sweet potatoes, and coleslaw. Several college-aged guys and gals were wandering the restaurant offering additional sides and throwing hot rolls. It dawned on me that it was Halloween when I saw one of the guys had a football jersey on and was acting like he was tossing a pigskin rather than mouthwatering starch. The meal was awesome, the service was friendly, and of course I made purchases at the gift store on the way out. Who wouldn't want a sixty-four-ounce pop guzzler and a stress ball in the shape of a toasted roll—which actually looked more like butt cheeks?

Though I wished I could take a food-induced nap instead of drive on, drive I did. Passed many herds of beef cattle, which made me feel funny about the lunch I just ate. (I'm quite conflicted on the whole vegetarian thing . . .) I recalled from my youth that there was a large McDonald's that spanned the freeway in Oklahoma; would I again stop and delay my progress? Of course! Once I arrived, it was not quite like I remembered it when I visited at age thirteen, but I did buy a Route 66 T-shirt at the gift shop.

Around eight thirty, when I seemed to be maxed out on driving, I rolled into the sleepy, quiet town of Shamrock, Texas. There wasn't much to choose from in the way of lodging, so I picked the one with the brightest outdoor lights. (Hey - a young woman alone at night in a strange town with truckers around - gotta play it safe.) I checked in with a young Arab man and settled in my second-floor room for the night. Because I'm a curious person, I checked the desk and nightstand for "supplies" (free pens, pad of paper, the usual stuff). I laughed hard and loud when a Mormon Bible looked up at me from the drawer. The irony was just too much: Shamrock, Texas (Irish) + Arab kid in the office + Mormon Bible. Are you kidding me? Was I spending the night in the Twilight Zone? I was too tired to care.

I departed Leprechaun Land at seven on November 1. It was a sunny morning, 51 degrees, and my odometer read 7,009 miles. As I headed west, I passed many wind turbines. I don't understand how they harness energy; it's a big mystery to me. I spotted many more cow fields and also located another Stuckey's, where I filled up the gas tank and got a snack. Land masses started to appear in the form of buttes rising up from the vast and arid scenery. Red dirt as well as striations in the rocks brought a smile to my face as the miles rolled by and the scenery changed. I actually saw tumbleweeds blowing! Prickly pears and yuccas decorated the roadside. Suddenly I wished I could drive a Jeep Wrangler through the fields, four-by-four style. Alas . . .

I ate some lunch and later I just couldn't help pulling into a touristy Indian gift shop. It took me way too long to decide on a piece of jewelry—silver and turquoise earrings—and a small dream catcher. The Native American salesman at the register was friendly and chatty. Around Moriarty, New Mexico, I noticed many trailers in the uneven fields, most of which looked not-so-appealing. I wondered if the local Native American population lived in those or the white population? Either way, it was rather depressing.

I made a thirty-minute stop in Albuquerque because my best friend said I had to. So I parked in Old Town and walked around the shops. Because I had already bought my touristy stuff for the day and hoped to make quite a bit more driving progress, I left town after taking a few photos.

It was dusk when I reached Winslow, Arizona. As an Eagles fan, I simply could not live with myself if I didn't stand on the corner made famous by their song "Take It Easy." The scene was much different from what I pictured, as things often are. Winslow is a small town, yet the famous corner was rather difficult to find. (Hello: Chamber of Commerce, *wake up!* Signs, please!) There was nothing but a statue of a guy standing on the corner, smiling. Since I was the only soul around, I couldn't get a photo *with* him, but of course I took one *of* him. Yet again, I hit up the tourist shop on the corner, full of Route 66 and Eagles paraphernalia.

It was past my normal stopping time of eight thirty–ish, and I still had about a two-hour drive to Vegas. I was getting punchy, frustrated, and tired. It was dark, and I didn't like driving in the dark in unfamiliar areas. After a five-minute meltdown in my car at a well-lit gas station who knows where, I pulled it together and just sped on. And on. And on. I went into autopilot, got in the zone, and kept driving. It was a very trying two hours for me personally. I unknowingly crossed the Hoover Dam in the dark (don't ask me how the signs didn't get my attention), followed the curves of the road, and *boom*—there appeared the valley of artificial light that contained Las Vegas. I had made it! My fifteen-hour day of driving was over. Woo hoo!

The La Quinta hotel I stayed at had a full hot breakfast every morning. Since the previous day drained me, I barely woke in time to pig out on waffles, OJ, coffee, fruit, and milk. I think I stole food for my room and the market basket in my car. Originally I had planned to spend this day – November 2 - hiking at Red Rock Canyon to the west of the city. But the weather was supposed to be better the following day, so I drove (back) to Hoover Dam instead, another of my bucket-list spots. It was a sunny day but very windy. The enormous site was pretty busy, with people of many nationalities visiting. The large scope of the dam was more than I imagined. I'm not into engineering or architecture, so I only spent about ninety minutes there. Science geeks could probably stay for hours.

Back in town, I thought a nap sounded good, so I indulged. After some slumber, I walked to the Miracle Mile Shops on the Strip. I had promised myself to only purchase local products while on my journey and not go regular retail shopping. But this was Vegas—nothing is regular there! I found an age-appropriate (and more importantly, price-appropriate) store with cute fashions and made a few frugal purchases. I started to feel tired again, so back to the hotel I went, in the dark, clutching my purse and purchases as I walked a mile down Paradise Road alone. Dinner was Chef Boyardee in a can, in my room, with the plastic picnic-ware I brought "just in case." I channel-surfed from the bed for a bit and was out.

The morning of November 3, the hotel breakfast lounge was crazy busy. Then I remembered there was some kind of event at the convention center that had brought thousands of people into town. I eventually got a seat at a table and filled up on grub. It was Red Rock Day! Hiking shoes: check! Walking pole: check! Sunglasses and snacks: check! GPS: you know it.

The freeway system in Las Vegas was surprisingly easy to navigate. I located the park with no problem. Red Rock Canyon contains a thirteen-mile scenic drive with many little parking lots where people can stop and take pictures or take a short hike to get closer to the wildlife and rocks. The scenery and landscape changed every few feet along the drive as each twist or bend brought a new landform into view. The rock colors were beautiful: dark orange, peach, yellow, white, and grey. Some rocks were in the shape of buttes; some were rugged and menacingly steep while others were rounded. They blended into each other like bubbles overflowing from a washing machine. I was in awe.

Although I had been to Phoenix in 2009 and hiked in the Superstition Mountains, I had not seen the landscapes I was now experiencing. This was a different type of Southwest topography. I pulled over at every parking lot for pictures or to take a short panoramic video. I wanted proof that I had been here, so I asked some folks to take pictures of me amidst the rocks. People were very kind. I followed one hiking trail for a short while, but it was very rocky (and I mean *rocks*—like the size of your head). I figured a sprained ankle could put a damper on my travel plans, so I carefully headed back to my car.

At one lot, there was not a soul present. I decided this was where I would eat my fiber bar and apple for lunch. I copped a squat on a large round rock near my car, faced the open southwesterly view, and shut my eyes. Quiet. The only noise was that of the fresh light breeze and the insects and birds in the canyon. That coupled with the warm midday sun on my face and body put me in a meditative state. *This is what I hope heaven is like*, I remember thinking. Blissed out.

The jaunt to Red Rock lasted approximately four hours. I aimlessly drove back to the hotel, not in a hurry, and later headed out for dinner and a drink. I enjoyed the fountains at the Bellagio, their music and water movement bringing a brief calm to the busy Strip. Then I wandered inside to admire my beloved Dale Chihuly glass ceiling. The lobby lighting is amazing. Someday I *will* own a piece of his work! Someday . . . no matter how small it is or how old I am or what it costs.

The next morning, November 4, I decided I was done with Vegas. The Chevy odometer read 8,100 miles. It was another sunny day, 64 degrees—good for traveling. As I headed north out of the city, I passed an ugly mass of electrical towers, wires, and power plants. Once through that area, I was happy to see the openness of the desert once again, the unique colors and shapes of the earth showing off in the daylight. I loved the changing topography. I became quite good at taking digital photos while going eighty mph down the highway, but don't tell.

The wind picked up as the day went on. Used to the pleasant atmosphere and amenities of La Quinta, I found the Budget Host in Richfield, Utah, to be less than stellar. But in truth, a bed and shower was all I really needed, and I was learning to not be so snobbish about my standards. As long as there were no bugs or mice, I was good.

Friday morning, I took my time getting up and around. I left the hotel at nine thirty. It was cold outside at 32 degrees, and foggy with light snow on the mountains (which in the dark from the night before I hadn't realized even existed). With the odometer now at 8,400 miles, I rolled east out of Richfield, only to have it start snowing twenty minutes later. Winds picked up and salt trucks were spreading their goods. The temperature jumped around within a 10-degree range, probably because of changes in altitude. The land formations I was encountering made it hard to keep my focus on the road. More pictures . . .

That feeling I'd had at Red Rock Canyon resurfaced. I was happy, at peace, awestruck, and feeling fortunate to be on such a trip. Every bend in the highway added another layer to my awe. I couldn't keep the smile off my face for stretches of road, and sometimes the views (along with the emotions I was experiencing) made me laugh and/or cry.

I was sad to be heading east toward Michigan—I loved what this solo journey was allowing me. The notion of going home and living in a boring state with a dead economy and a societal "box" really scared me. A latent insatiable craving to see, learn, explore, and experience places, food, cultures, and geography had been released. How could I pack that away in a closet and just proceed with my mundane life?

By noon, I had reached the Moab area in eastern Utah. It was still windy out, which, along with the cloudy sky, caused it to feel colder than the 52 degrees my car thermometer displayed. My goal: Arches National Park. I made some purchases in the gift shop before beginning the drive through the park. I was trying to buy locally made products whenever I could, and here I bought an eight-by-ten-inch watercolor of one of the park's arches, painted by a local artist. Whenever I look at that, to this day, I am transported back to the vast red land and the cloudy, windy weather.

Much like Red Rock, Arches was set up to be driven through, with pit stops for pictures mostly, not so much hiking. I was disappointed that it was so cloudy. I wanted pictures of land carvings that glowed orange in the sun's generous rays instead of images of ominous brownish holes. Maybe next time.

I diverged off the road many times to explore the formations noted on the park guide. Because of the time of day and my mileage goal, I spent about two and a half hours at Arches National Park. Let me tell you something: walking on such old rock and dirt, surrounded by amazing natural structures, the wind cleansing my lungs and messing my hair, I realized how big this world is, how vast God's imagination was in creating it, and how very small I am. If a person can fall in love with inanimate objects like rocks, then I left my heart in Moab.

By five thirty, I had reached Grand Junction in western Colorado. It was 44 degrees, and I noticed the clouds were thickening as the elevation rose. East of Grand Junction, I started to experience a significant amount of snowfall. My plan was to try to make it just east of Denver before stopping for the night. It was dark now and very scary on the roads; the state police were shutting down freeway entrance and exit ramps, and all of a sudden Denver didn't matter. I needed to hunker down somewhere for the night and *fast*. I drove for miles hoping to see a motel, but I was getting discouraged. Then I saw a neon vacancy sign at the Roost Lodge and immediately got off the strange service drive I somehow seemed to be on.

The motel's wood siding was painted brick red, made brighter by the crisp, heavy white snow all around it. In the car, I put my hiking shoes on, since I hadn't brought snow boots. The office was sparse and the guestroom was overpriced, but I was in a pickle in the Rockies, so they had me over a barrel. The room was probably the second worst of the entire trip. I didn't even want to walk on the old carpet in my bare feet. Anxiety kept me awake as I tried to unwind from the evening's events. I didn't know where I was or how long this storm would last. No cable reception on the TV meant no weather report.

The next morning, I discovered I was in Vail, Colorado. It was 24 degrees and overcast. The snow had stopped overnight; maybe three inches had accumulated. The view directly across from my second-floor window was of a sunny blue sky and fresh powdered ski runs with a cute village at the base. I had my free breakfast of stale cereal and burnt coffee in the office and then set off on foot to find out what the little village was all about, and hopefully get a real meal.

It was nine when I left the motel, and of course the shops didn't open until ten, so I wandered up and down the pedestrian-only streets of this shopping village, freezing my keister off. Got a *real* coffee and a scone at a wacky café, the only business open. Once the shops opened, I purchased a Vail hoodie sweatshirt, and then I started driving.

By midday, I reached the college town of Boulder. The sun was offset by a brisk wind. I parked and walked around Pearl Street Mall near the shadows of the Flatirons. Making my way through the unique shops and restaurants, I was in search of a warm hat, and finally found a colorful wool and fleece cap at a funky shop. I was hungry, but Boulder was so hip, I didn't want to look like a dork eating alone. Nor did I want to spend money on an overpriced meal. I wound up reverting back to car snacks instead.

The Chevy was in desperate need of a car wash (after driving through the salt and snow sludge) and an oil change. There were no retail chains like Pennzoil or Uncle Ed's Oil Shoppe in those parts. As I drove toward Kansas, the topography turned into flat, beige fields with hundreds of black cows. I was in the middle of absolutely nowhere. As it got dark, I was craving pizza something awful. I used an app on my iPhone to locate a Pizza Hut, and I was actually so close to one that I almost passed it! I ordered a personal pizza and pop, and mindlessly watched the news on TV while waiting. Oblivious to the time, I suddenly realized that I should have had my food served already. The friendly blond teenage boy who waited on me (he referred to me as "ma'am") promptly returned with my pizza and told me dinner was on the house since it took a bit long. I settled into Oakley, Kansas, for the night.

Monday, November 7, I departed Oakley at nine, still needing an oil change, with the odometer now reading 9,305. I pulled into a truck-stop late that morning and asked where a girl could get an oil change around the area. It just so happened there was a repair shop behind the station that normally serviced big rigs but would do a change for me. Yay! You know, besides having to be resourceful on this trip, I couldn't be afraid of being a lone female. I was on my guard and tried to make practical decisions, don't get me wrong. But I found that almost every person I encountered on the road had a smile for me and gladly answered my questions. That is something I found pleasantly surprising—people's kindness to strangers.

As I drove through the boring flat farmland of Kansas, I discovered more wind farms and cows—and apparently that the state is off the grid, because I had absolutely no phone signal. Now *that* was kinda scary! Driving in a steady rain for hours, I passed the Russell Stover candy plant in Abilene and went off-route to see the Oz Museum in Wamego. (Waste of time—it was really just a store. False advertising!) I had hoped to visit the Amelia Earhart Museum, but it was getting ready to close for the day as I was about to head in that direction. I bet it would have been better than Oz. That evening's hotel of choice was the Motel 6 in Columbia.

The morning of November 8 was cloudy and 62 degrees; the car odometer read 9,806 miles. I indulged in Starbucks for breakfast;

boy, was it appreciated after days without! When I reached St. Louis, Missouri around noon, I had time to snag a ride in the arch this time through town. I wanted to make it home by the end of the day, but when it comes to items on your bucket list, time doesn't matter—you pause for them.

The arch ride was running, and it wasn't even busy! I was so excited I was practically jumping out of my skin like a kid waiting for an amusement-park ride. There was a short line while guests waited for the "pods" to return so we could ride them up. Supposedly, they could seat five people, but I doubt that calculation. I was knee to knee with an older couple in our pod, just the three of us. It was all white inside and reminded me of Mork from Ork and his egg from the 1970s TV show. After the four minute ride up, I raced to the western windows to view downtown St. Louis. The floor and walls/windows were at funky angles, but that made it easy to take pictures. I was surprised to see a group of Amish wandering the viewing area. Was riding in futuristic pods allowed in their *Ordnung*?

Trying not to rush the experience, I stayed longer than some just to enjoy the feeling that there, in that moment, I was fulfilling yet another dream on this trip. The pod ride down the arch only took three minutes thanks to the pull of gravity. Passing through Kansas City around dinnertime was perfect, because I wanted to eat at the world-famous Arthur Bryant's BBQ. It wasn't busy either, but the food sure tasted good.

After dark, I got lost in the metro Indianapolis highway system. After freaking out a bit about driving in "the hood," not knowing which direction to head, my best friend who attended grad school there texted me and said, "Just head north." I was on some numbered side street, but I was driving north. Eventually I made it to Interstate 69, and by then I was so spent by the disorienting ordeal and the time and stress it cost me, I knew I had to stop for one more night, despite the fact that I was only about four hours from home.

I found a nice hotel that evening just east of Indy called the Sleep Inn. It had an indoor pool, which I was definitely going to use, and the sheets and bathroom didn't make me feel queasy. It was the most money I'd paid for a hotel on the trip, but I figured I deserved some comforts and a clean environment on my last evening of Road Trip 2011.

The free breakfast was a close second to that of the La Quinta in Vegas. I ate until I knew I had eaten too much. After a good night's sleep and various breakfast items, it was time for the home stretch. The weather was rainy, windy, and 56 degrees. I left shortly after seven, I think—time zones were hard to keep track of—with an odometer reading of 10,230 miles. Within two hours, I had crossed the Michigan state line. This made me happy because I was tired: tired of the last three days of rain, tired of crappy though affordable motels, and tired of an irregular eating schedule. But I was more sad that this crazy, awesome, unstructured journey was ending. The weather was gloomy, and so was I. The question popped into my brain: *How can I adjust back to normal Michigan life after all that I've seen and experienced?* The answer was to incorporate the trip and all that came with it into my life, for enrichment and growth.

To help me remember some of what I learned on the trip, I wrote a list, and this is it, verbatim:

- Good navigation skills.
- Can take photos from a moving vehicle!
- Snow, sleet, and ice on the curvy Rocky Mountain roads? No problem!
- If you don't set any expectations, you won't be disappointed.
- Impulse is as important as having a plan.

- It moves and angers me that the US government stole Native American land. Driving through New Mexico, Arizona, and Utah was sad for me that way.
- Quietness of my soul—blank mind.
- In the moment.
- I can do what I think I can't when I push myself.
- Curiosity is my lifeline.
- Mountains are amazing!
- I don't like being manipulated, misled, or "marketed."
- Require an equal balance of freedom and structure.
- Confidence in my choices; being in control of myself.

That road trip changed me. I could feel it as I was on the journey, and I still feel its effects. It changed how I saw myself and how I viewed strangers. I learned what pleased and displeased me and what boosted my confidence. Most of all, it confirmed what I'd suspected for years: I am a traveler full of wanderlust. Just give me a map and some resources, and I shall willingly go exploring.

Confucius is quoted as saying, "Wherever you go, go with all your heart." I did, absolutely. And will again.

Chapter 11

Field Trip

Once in a while, a person just needs to get out of Dodge, you know? And I mean that literally, since Detroit makes them.

It was early September 2012, and the wanderlust hit me hard once again. On a whim, I chose to take a late summer/early fall drive to central New York state, where I had a friend and two bucket-list destinations I wanted to check off. Since I was unemployed and on limited income, I thought it best to camp at a New York state park for fifteen dollars per night rather than stay at a chain hotel for nearly a hundred dollars per night. Off I went to the sporting-goods store for a small tent, sleeping pad (to absorb moisture from the ground), and tarp. Total cost: sixty dollars.

Leaving metro Detroit in my Chevy just after noon on a sunny day, I realized I would be setting up my campsite in the dark. The sun would set around eight thirty, and I anticipated at least a nine-hour drive. Now, before I proceed, you must be advised: I have only ever camped in a travel trailer before, and never alone. Add to that the bonus of a sprained wrist—for which I wore a Velcro splint day and night—and the more I thought about it, the more I realized I *hadn't* thought. Oh well, spontaneous adventures aren't often the most delicately planned events.

I did have enough smarts to pack nonperishable food items, fruit, bottled water, and juices, as well as mace, flares, essential camping items in a dry box, my passport (since I was taking a shortcut through Ontario), and maps. The previous year, I had taken my eleven-day road trip out west and back by myself, so I was not afraid of traveling alone again. This three-day trip would be fun.

All was well for about two hours. I entered Canada uneventfully at customs, but then my cheap GPS wouldn't work outside the United States. I used the tracking map on my cell phone, unaware that I did not have international cellular service and was being charged extra fees the entire time I was in Ontario. When the billing statement arrived later on, it reflected a ninety dollar international fee. Wanting to avoid the likely crowded major freeway and in an effort to see the countryside, I opted for a different route, where I got lost on some crazy unnamed or triple-named zigzag country roads that cut through one-stoplight towns in the middle of dairy land. I finally got my bearings and was grateful to cross the border into Buffalo. Immediately after entering I-90, I exited to pee and eat. I figured I wouldn't have to stop again.

As the sun slowly set over the increasing hilly, green terrain surrounding I-90, I realized it was not such a boring drive. The sparse exits did freak me out just a little. But the euphoric freedom of the open road I had felt the previous year had returned, and again I felt that this was somehow the real me: Stacy the Adventurer. Eleven dollars in tolls later, I exited toward Rome, New York, near my campground. Even with my car GPS now working, I didn't trust it, so I stuck to the phone navigation. I traveled down odd little highways (not the kind I'm used to, anyway) to two-lane roads that curved way back into nowhere, in the dark, with no streetlights. Once in a while, I saw a small green sign on the side of the road indicating I was indeed headed toward the state park.

When I pulled into the park, it was after ten o'clock, and the ranger station was closed. Since I'd preregistered for my reserved spot earlier online (while "roaming" in Canada), I had no need to check in. Without a park map, I drove around and followed arrows until I located my site. It was totally dark; even the few nearby campers had already turned their lights off. Shortly after pulling onto my site, a junior ranger (and I say "junior" because he seemed fresh out of Land Maintenance school, which made him *at least* a dozen years my junior) drove by my site, verified that I had registered online, asked my name, and bid me a good evening.

I left my car running with the high beams aimed at where I would assemble my living quarters. There were no occupied sites across from me in my section of the park, so I wasn't blinding anyone. No one was burning a campfire, and the only thing I smelled was the fresh air of the woods at night and a body of water nearby. Even the animals were silent.

I unpacked the camping equipment from my trunk, briefly read the tent-assembly instructions (I had seen many demonstrations on annual family camping trips), and got to work. First I unwrapped the tarp and placed it on the ground where I wanted my tent to be. Then I unzipped the pouch containing my tent. As it turned out, I had unknowingly reserved a spot with the rockiest and hardest ground, and the small metal spikes took *forever* to drive into the dense earth with my plastic mallet. I'm talking forty-five minutes. I felt bad for my few fellow campers; I hope my incessant pounding and swearing didn't keep them up. I proceeded to have issues with the shock poles and threading them through all the right loops and pouches. After several attempts, the tent was more or less stable. It's a good thing mild, calm weather was predicted; otherwise, I don't think the tent would have stayed up and in place. My wrist was killing me from hammering the stakes into the rubble. And I was tired from driving.

Luckily, the bathhouse was a stone's throw away; I could see its faint light across a few vacant sites. Grabbing my small lantern lest I come across and scare a skunk (which would just *so* not make my day), I walked swiftly toward the only evidence of modernization. Old but in decent condition, the bathhouse had no showers, only toilets and sinks. *Great*, I thought. *Where the heck am I supposed to shower? A truck stop on I-90?*

I crawled into my cozy navy-and-yellow tent where I slept like a rock (pun intended). My bedroll and sleeping bag kept me warm during the cool evening. After daylight arrived, I groggily rubbed my eyes, yet was bursting with anticipation to view my surroundings in the light of day. I listened to the sound of the woods waking for a moment before I had to rush outside to the toilets.

When I unzipped and crawled out of my tiny flap door, I was immediately gazing upon a beautiful late-morning sunrise, the light dancing on the surface of the lake. The campground was pretty much all wooded, and with so few campers it was a quiet delight to greet the day. Various unidentified birds sang their songs, squirrels and chipmunks called out to lay claim to their food sources, and I grabbed my small digital camera and slipped on my flip-flops before scurrying to the lavatory and then heading to the lakeshore, which was just across the road from me. Trees of all kinds bordered the expansive lake, enclosing it in their protective boughs. I started snapping photos with my camera, and then I had to stop and forcefully remind myself to "stop and smell the roses," so to speak. Too often I was obsessed with getting what I thought to be the perfect shot, when what would make that moment in time stand out in my memory better was just sitting still, quieting my brain, and being in the beautiful moment.

I gathered toiletries and headed to the facilities, not knowing quite what to do since I couldn't take a shower. I definitely needed one! The door to the 1960s restroom didn't lock, so any of the few women in my camping circle could walk in on me at any second, but I had no choice: part by part, I would quickly strip, wash, dry, and re-dress. In a frantic panic, I quickly took the oddest bath of my life. Washing my hair in a porcelain sink smaller than my laptop proved to be the most challenging part. I should have done this task first, as I was half wet by the time I was finished. Back in my tent, I dressed and primped for the day (as much as I could), had a snack, and went in search of coffee on the way to meet up with a friend for lunch.

I pulled into the small parking lot in front of my friend's guitar store, turned the car off, and realized I was crazy for driving all this way. But I had been looking forward to seeing him and the awesome gear at the store. Stepping through the door, I was overwhelmed by gorgeous and colorful electric guitars, numerous pedals, and an insane amount of amps and basses, all neatly displayed. Suddenly my claim as a novice acoustic player meant nothing.

My friend was sitting in the front lobby area, and he invited me to sit down and chat. A few regular customers stopped by, breaking up our conversation. When a lull came, my friend declared it was lunchtime and walked me a few doors down to a mom-and-pop-type hamburger/shake joint. After he treated me to lunch, we walked back to the store, where he gave me some CDs, a T-shirt, and smaller miscellaneous items to take back to Michigan with me. The few hours at the store flew by, and I could have stayed longer, but wanted to see the Baseball Hall of Fame and Museum before it closed for the day. My friend walked me to my car and gave me a hug. I was sad to leave.

It was almost an hour's drive to the quaint Americana village of Cooperstown. The drive was full of views of lakes and rolling green hills, and the town itself was idyllic with its mature trees, American flags on display, and well-kept older homes. I quickly parked near the museum, realizing I had roughly an hour to zip through its exhibits before closing. The greeter was kind enough to only charge me half of the normal admittance fee since I arrived so late in the day. Again, it was a battle within me whether to take pictures or just enjoy the moment. I tried my best to do both. I sought out specific displays and sections, avoiding some that weren't of real personal interest. The displays in the "Baseball in the Movies" section were cool; I'm a huge fan of *The Natural* and *A League of Their Own*. I was pleased to see some former Detroit Tiger players in the Hall of Fame. The last ten minutes were spent at the gift shop choosing souvenirs for people back home (okay . . . and *me*). After the museum closed, I walked up and down the short main street, peeking into storefront and restaurant windows and taking a few pictures. I grabbed a bite at a cute yet unfriendly diner.

As I drove back toward Utica, I was craving a beer and perhaps something sweet. So I parked next to an Italian restaurant, went inside, and after about twenty minutes of waiting, placed and received my drink order (Utica Club, a local craft beer)—only to never be waited on again, despite direct eye contact with waitstaff and trying to grab them in passing. I am not one of those people who is embarrassed to do much of anything alone, but I started to feel a bit self-conscious sitting alone at my table in this small restaurant.

After an hour of no service, I waved my arms and flagged a waiter down, saying I'd like my check. He asked if I wanted anything to eat, seeing only my empty beer glass on the table. I replied that I would have loved some food, but no one waited on me to take my order, and I really just wanted to get out of there and waste no more of my evening. He ran around a minute, returned to my table, apologized, and said my beer was on the house, to which I replied loudly, "Good—it should be!" I swiftly grabbed my jacket from the back of the chair, put it on in one big flourish, grabbed my purse, and bolted from that snobby place. It was now dark as I headed back to camp, still craving a sweet. I stopped at a gas station and got a candy bar, a bitter consolation prize.

I set my alarm for an early morning, but I must have hit the snooze or off button, because I got up later than I would have liked. Still without a park map, I decided to drive around, thinking there *must* be a shower somewhere. You don't even know the relief I felt when I saw a sign and the building for the bathhouse! I couldn't linger—I had camp to break down still—but the hot water felt soooo good falling on my skin after the previous day's awkward morning cleanup experience. Sometimes it's the small things that make me happy.

Returning to my site, I disassembled camp in record speed, impressing even myself. Known as a master packer, I swept out, wiped down, and packed everything neatly in my trunk for the long drive back to Michigan. I pulled off of my site at exactly 11:00 a.m., the required departure time, and I drove to the park's public beach, which had a lovely view of Delta Lake. With hardly any campers around, it was so quiet—I just wanted to dig out a towel and lie on the sand, soak up some vitamin D, and enjoy the Zen-like environment around me for a few hours. Instead, I removed my shoes, rolled up my jeans, walked out to the beach area, and waded through the muck near the shore to the shallow lake water. Although there was an early fall chill, the sun was shining, and it would have been a perfect day and location to kayak. I regretted not reserving one more day, strapping my kayak to the Chevy roof, and adding that adventure to my New York valley experience.

Driving west on I-90, I had my mind set on visiting the Susan B. Anthony House in Rochester, New York. I pulled into the small parking lot next to her home/museum, full of excitement. The guided walking tour was very informative, and I fully appreciated Ms. Anthony's passion and sacrifice. The docent informed me of her burial location, and I felt compelled to find it and visit her grave as well. It was on the other side of town at Mt. Hope Cemetery, where fellow activist Frederick Douglass was also buried. As I turned into one of the many entrances to this expansive hallowed ground, I was awestruck by its size—several city blocks long and wide. It is the resting place for approximately 350,000 persons. Once I entered the grounds, as far as my eyes could see were headstones of varying sizes or mausoleums, and tiny metal signs identifying parcels or blocks. How on earth was I going to locate these two graves in such a vast space? Google.

I found Frederick Douglass's tombstone first, as there was an easily-spotted marker on the one-lane road. I parked partially on the grass, grabbed my raincoat, and followed other signs as I traipsed through the grounds that took me to his burial spot. Such a large and imposing memorial for this man of historical measure! There was a small American flag at the corner of his site. I stood staring at the marker with his name on it, dwelling on what his life must have been like and how hard he worked for his cause. There were leaves that had collected on the flat gravestone, and I gingerly brushed them away, talking under my breath to this ghost of a man as I did so.

As I headed back to my car, it began to drizzle. Now to find Ms. Anthony. The directions were so poor within the park, I drove around for at least thirty minutes searching for her section, which I located from online sources. I finally stumbled upon it, quite literally, after climbing a hill to which there was no road access. It was raining harder and getting windy and cold. I searched the section until I found the *family* plot. Her father had a large Anthony marker (of course) and her mother and siblings surrounded him. Susan was at the front left corner, with a small and unassuming rounded upright headstone. There was a flag at her grave also, along with a small container of yellow roses.

After just being at her home not two hours earlier, I had a lot to reflect on as I crouched there in the cold rain. I thanked her for her determination and sacrifices, for her boldness and vision. She was a feminist before feminism was revolutionized. I pondered her life with its varying complexities and seemingly unwavering boldness. I spent more time with her than I did taking pictures. I owed her, and myself, that much. I carefully descended the slippery hill down to my car, bidding adieu to a new hero.

Aware of the late hour (approximately five o'clock), I was discouraged by the long drive yet ahead of me, but I wouldn't have traded those past few hours for anything. During rush hour, I found my way back to I-90 West, got a sandwich and some gas at a rest stop on the turnpike, and proceeded toward Canada. There was a bit of a wait at the border, even with several lanes open. When I finally rolled up to the booth, I was faced with a young, cute border officer who kindly informed me that mace was illegal in Canada. I honestly insisted that when I'd entered the country two days earlier, the lady had asked no questions, just let me through. He frowned and said he could seize it and have me detained and searched, but if I drove straight through to the other US border with no overnight stays, he would let me go. He also advised that if I made any stops, to hide the mace in the trunk instead of the glove box. I thanked him profusely and hurried on my way, this time sticking to highways and not rural detours.

The longer I drove, the more tired and punchy I felt. Based on last year's road trip, I knew my limits, and I had just about reached them. Another four hours of driving was not in the cards. I realized I would have no choice but to stay the night in Ontario, something I did *not* want to do—nor did the border cutie want me to do. But it was that or risk being a dangerously tired driver. I located a decent motel right off a highway exit. I would have to get up *really* early the next day, because I was scheduled to participate in a Walk to End Alzheimer's near home.

The next morning I awoke, showered, ate some free breakfast, and sped toward Sarnia with a watchful eye for cops. The line for this border crossing was even longer than the one the previous night. Nervously, I waited in the queue, not wanting to be late or miss my charity walk. After twenty minutes, I was cleared. I set my cruise control on a number I won't disclose and made it to the charity walk just as it was starting.

I left Michigan restless and returned tired but pleased with my whirlwind, productive, and meaningful journey. Though it wasn't flawless, I was proud of my solo camping prowess. It was good to see my friend and Cooperstown, and to learn more about Susan B. Anthony. My wanderlust was grounded, at least for a few months.

Epilogue

It was difficult for me to stop writing this book, as I found there were more and more stories I wanted to add. Probably a plague for novice memoirists. I tried to quit while I was still ahead.

There are situations that have changed since their occurrence or my writing of them. Dynamics of some family and friend relationships have since altered, but this memoir is about my life—how I have viewed and experienced it—not anyone else's. The chapters contained in this collection are snapshots of places, people, time, and circumstances told as they were experienced by me at that point.

Afterword

I have dabbled in writing my entire life. In elementary school, I won a local award for a story with the theme of acceptance and learning from other cultures. For many of my school years, I kept a daily diary to clear my mind of school and home turmoil. High-school teachers prompted my interest in writing to grow, and I worked for the school paper, aced creative-writing assignments, and wrote poems constantly.

My creative side took a hiatus during my twenties when I thought working full-time and being a wife was all there was to life. Then I enrolled in community college and the ideas, concepts, and words began to flow once more, encouraged by my professor and friend, John Corbin. I contributed to the college arts journal, with my work being approved and commended by the head of the English department.

After graduation, I hit a rough patch and felt that I wanted, *needed*, to work on a project. I had to have an outlet for what was circling around inside my head and binding my heart. My close friend Erik had lunch with me in December 2011 and, hearing my frustrations, asked why I couldn't write again. What was stopping me? I confessed that it seemed there was so much to say that I wasn't sure where or how to start. His response, spoken with a grin, was, "There's your opening line."

Although I did not use it as my opening line, that sentence was a constant push for me to proceed, no matter how difficult the words were to type or how long it took to tell the story right. His faith and confidence in me and my abilities motivated and encouraged me, and here is the end product.

About the Author

Stacy Rose Bowen is a Michigan native. Her interests and passions include writing, animals, travel, hiking, music, reading, kayaking, and photography. Stacy is a graduate of Oakland Community College with a major in liberal arts.

Her previous published work includes several poems and short stories featured in Oakland Community College's annual academic arts journal, *The Speakeasy*, and a few online articles.

When not planning the next trip to calm her wanderlust, Stacy can be found at her laptop with a cup of coffee and a sleeping cat nearby.

This is her first book.

www.ingramcontent.com/pod-product-compliance
Ingram Content Group UK Ltd.
Pitfield, Milton Keynes, MK11 3LW, UK
UKHW020128250726
13967UKWH00002B/538